How to Understand the Bible

Mel is a thoughtful analyst of church life today. Best of all—he actually does what he writes about.

—John Ortberg, author and pastor

Having known Mel Lawrenz for thirty-five years in various capacities as student, intern, colleague, and eventual successor as senior pastor of Elmbrook Church, I can testify to his keen mind, his profound respect for and knowledge of history, his forward-looking curiosity, his undoubted communication gifts, and his many years as a seasoned practitioner of church ministry.

—Stuart Briscoe, author and pastor

Mel Lawrenz's vision of a local church that actually reflects the wholeness and beauty of God as it engages with the Lord, one another, and the community is a much-needed call back to God's original Plan A – a plan that has too often been cast aside in the name of specialization, church growth, and expediency.

—Larry Osborne, author and pastor

HOW TO
UNDERSTAND

THE
BIBLE

MEL LAWRENZ

WWW.WORDWAY.ORG

Cover and interior design: Sheila Hahn

To Win, who loves God and loves that God has spoken.

CONTENTS

Part IV. Interpreting the Bible

To the Reader

Whether you are just starting to read the Bible or have been reading it for decades, it is always helpful to step back and gain some perspective on why we do this, and how we should do it.

By "how to" I do not mean approaching Bible reading in a mechanical way. If Scripture is the word of God, then reading it is an intimate, dynamic, mind-bending, soul-shaking experience—anything but mechanical. The "how-to's" of this process include knowing the historical background of the portion we are reading, and knowing how words work: the difference between a psalm and a proverb, the special characteristics of epistles, the power of prophecy, the extraordinary teaching methods of Jesus, and so on.

I wanted this book to be short and practical. If you are motivated to go on to larger works about Bible backgrounds and interpretation, that's great. But having been a pastor for quite a few years, I know that a great many people have yet to read an introductory survey about understanding the Bible. This compact book is a beginning orientation.

How to Understand the Bible: A Simple Guide is not one person's interpretation of what the Bible means, but a guide for how to prepare yourself and orient yourself for reading Scripture. Knowing Scripture is about knowing God. In it is a lifetime of discoveries.

For supplemental resources for
individuals and groups:

www.WordWay.org

Part I

APPROACHING THE BIBLE

Chapter 1

HOW CAN WE UNDERSTAND THE BIBLE BETTER?

If you wish you understood the Bible better, you're in good company.

It is not just newcomers reading the Bible for the first time who think the Bible can be challenging to understand. Mature believers think that. Bible scholars think that. Even biblical writers thought that. Second Peter 3:16 says: "[The apostle Paul's] letters contain some things that are hard to understand."

This should not surprise us. It should, instead, enthuse us and inspire us. It should fuel our curiosity and compel us to worship. If, when we hold a Bible in our hands, we have the word of the Creator of the universe—a Creator who loves us so much that he chooses not to leave us in silence—then we should not be surprised that it can be mysterious, complex, and deep.

We should not want it any other way.

If the Bible were as easy to understand as a news magazine or someone's blog, then God would not be greater than a journalist or a blogger. If we could understand all of the Bible the first year we read it, what more would there be for us for the rest of our lives? If the Bible did not take some work and patience to grasp, how could it possibly be a reliable guide for the great challenges of our lives? Think of it this way: if you went to a great banquet where there was a 30-foot-long buffet table with dozens of different foods, you would not be discouraged if you walked away having tasted only some of the amazing foods there. You would, instead, be enthused to return to it another day in order to taste more.

The Bible is challenging because it challenges. Mark Twain put it this way: "It ain't those parts of the Bible that I can't understand that bother me, it is the parts that I do understand." The word of God is wonderfully subversive. Scripture is like the scalpel that cuts, but also like a salve that heals. No empire or civilization can suppress the truth of the word of God because:

> He sits enthroned above the circle of the earth,
> and its people are like grasshoppers.
> He stretches out the heavens like a canopy,

and spreads them out like a tent to live in.
(Isa. 40:22)

This is the God who has spoken—to us.

Vast numbers of people respect the Bible, but they long to understand it better. That includes people who have read the Bible for many years, and those who have been hesitant even to try. Here is great news: The Bible, written by many authors over many years, and believed to be the word of God by billions of people, is God talking to the human race. And God wants to be understood.

The Bible is God's word in human words. The prophets and apostles were real people, urgently proclaiming, teaching, correcting, and warning. These writers of Scripture meant specific things in what they said.

If the Bible has stood the test of time across the ages and within thousands of different cultures, then we can be sure that this word of God will prove reliable for any circumstance of our lives.

This small book, *How to Understand the Bible: A Simple Guide*, is not an argument for the authority of the Bible—a topic covered ably by many other books. This book is a concise and practical guidebook for any believer wishing to read the Bible and understand it as the word of God—to understand what God is saying in it. It is meant to encourage and enthuse you, and motivate you to feed on this truth. As Psalm 34:8 says, "Taste and see that the LORD is good." The great prospect of better understanding the Bible is that we also come to understand God better.

And that is why God spoke in the first place.

So this is how, in this small book, we'll walk through the question of understanding the Bible. First, some questions on "Approaching the Bible," like "What is the big picture of the Bible?" "What about translations?" "What help can we get so we understand the Bible better?" etc. Next, we'll answer basic questions about "Understanding the Old Testament," to be followed by "Understanding the New Testament." Finally, we'll say some things about "Interpreting the Bible."

We'll begin with a question of motivation: "How will our lives be better if we understand the Bible better?"

Chapter 2

HOW WILL OUR LIVES BE BETTER IF WE UNDERSTAND THE BIBLE BETTER?

It is fair to ask the question: "How will my life be better if I understand the Bible better?" because it certainly is possible to own a Bible, carry a Bible, read the Bible, listen to Bible teachings and sermons, and neglect working to understand what the Bible actually means. It is worth everything to understand the Bible better.

First, understanding the Bible *leads to a fruitful life*. The very first words of the very first Psalm say this:

> Blessed is the one
>   who does not walk in step with the wicked
> or stand in the way that sinners take

or sit in the company of mockers,
but whose delight is in the law of the LORD,
    and who meditates on his law day and night.
That person is like a tree planted by streams
    of water,
    which yields its fruit in season
and whose leaf does not wither—
    whatever they do prospers. (Ps. 1:1-3)

We need to be intentional about what kind of people we are. Do we want to be "planted" in a place of health and fruitfulness, or to wander in sin and even wickedness?

One day Jesus taught that understanding and applying his words *leads to a stable life.*

"Everyone who hears these words of mine and puts them into practice is like a wise man who built his house on the rock. The rain came down, the streams rose, and the winds blew and beat against that house; yet it did not fall, because it had its foundation on the rock." (Matt. 7:24-25)

Jesus' words are at the core of the word of God, but they must be understood and lived. Building your house on the sand of human opinion, popular sentiment, or arbitrary expertise leads to one outcome only... to be washed away.

The apostle Paul explains how the word of God *leads to a quality life.*

> All Scripture is God-breathed and is useful for teaching, rebuking, correcting and training in righteousness, so that the servant of God may be thoroughly equipped for every good work. (2 Tim. 3:16-17)

What an enormous blessing it is to have Holy Scripture, breathed out by God, which does these four things: (1) teaching (that is, telling us the truth), (2) rebuking (that is, telling us when we're off track in our lives), 3) correcting (that is, getting us back on track), and (4) training in righteousness (that is, helping us stay on track). This is quality control for our lives. It is God speaking to us in all candor, honesty, support, and confrontation. It is the firm hand of discipline with the gentle touch of love.

Love is really why we have Scripture—why God breaks the silence and silences the noise. The writer of Hebrews put it best:

> In the past God spoke to our ancestors through the prophets at many times and in various ways, but in these last days he has spoken to us by his Son, whom he appointed heir of all things, and through whom also he made the universe. The Son is the

radiance of God's glory and the exact representation of his being, sustaining all things by his powerful word. After he had provided purification for sins, he sat down at the right hand of the Majesty in heaven. (Heb. 1:1-3)

The major turning points in the Bible are not merely history. They are acts of love—God building God's own story exactly how he wanted it. The law of the Old Testament is God patiently teaching human beings about holiness. The prophets screamed their warnings and proclaimed great promise—both acts of love. And then came God's speech through his Son. In Jesus we get truth, which is greater than just "truths." The Son is radiance, glory, purification, authority. Those red letters we read in the Gospels are not moralistic maxims. They are piercing beams of light.

How will our lives be better if we understand the Bible better?

When I was a teenager and a brand-new believer, I was in a Christian coffeehouse where someone taught a while, and then someone sang for a bit, and all of us sat around rustic round tables talking about life. A young man at my table who was a few years older than me had with him an enormous Bible, almost the size of what you see on altars in churches, with wooden covers and gilded edges. I will never forget him looking me dead in the eye and saying, "Whatever else you do—pay attention to the words of this book. It has everything you need." I will never forget that huge Bible, the intense look of conviction in the eyes of that young man, and his simple, focused admonition. From that moment on, I read Scripture differently, with eyes of faith. I felt like the Bible was reading me, rather than me reading the Bible, which exposed me to a power—benevolent, consistent, and constructive—I had never known before.

Chapter 3

WHAT IS THE BIG PICTURE OF THE BIBLE?

If you walked into someone's home, picked a big book off a shelf, and read a single line on a random page, one thing is certain: you would not understand it. That is because *we receive meaning through words by seeing them in their context.*

One of the most helpful things we can do to understand the Bible better is to gain a clear comprehension of the whole sweep of the biblical text. To see "the big picture." Grabbing a verse here and there for life meaning is like saying to God that we will only listen to him if he uses Twitter to send us tweets.

No, the Bible is a vast, epic story. The story of God, and the story of humanity.

The Hebrew Scriptures (what Christians call "The Old Testament") are a collection of writings that dozens of authors wrote over hundreds of years. It is breathtaking. The books of the Old Testament include history, prophecy, poetry, wisdom, and law.

The Pentateuch ("five books")—Genesis, Exodus, Leviticus, Numbers, and Deuteronomy—tell the story of beginnings. The creation of the universe, the fall of humanity into sin and corruption, the development of humanity. We learn about the character of God, a personal God who uses a particular family to show how he would work through covenant. He is the God of Abraham, Isaac, and Jacob. Out of love God delivered this people from slavery (Exodus), gave them definition for life (the commandments and laws), and brought them eventually to a land of their own.

The 12 books of history that follow (Joshua, Judges, Ruth, 1 and 2 Samuel, 1 and 2 Kings, 1 and 2 Chronicles, Ezra, Nehemiah, and Esther) continue the story of God with humanity. This is not history in the modern sense of facts and statistics. It is a true drama filled with tenderness and violence, success and failure, faithfulness and unfaithfulness. Hundreds of thousands of descendants of Abraham enter the land of promise, they struggle to live under God's authority since the lure of sin is always so strong. So they install a king and a government like the other nations. But after merely three generations, the kingdom becomes divided and the following 200 years are full of disappointments broken up with occasional revivals. Eventually the superpowers from the regions to the northeast—Assyria and then Babylonia—sweep down on the divided kingdom. They destroy, they exile. But after five decades, small numbers of Hebrews are allowed to return to rebuild their community and their nation.

Next, we have the books of Poetry and Wisdom: Job, Psalms, Proverbs, Ecclesiastes, and Song of Songs. The authors of these books let loose praise, anguish, affirmation, and longing. We learn much here about what is in the human heart, and in the heart of God.

The books called the Major Prophets (Isaiah, Jeremiah, Lamentations, Ezekiel, and Daniel) and the 12 Minor Prophets (Hosea, Joel, Amos, Obadiah, Jonah, Micah, Nahum, Habakkuk, Zephaniah, Haggai, Zechariah, and Malachi) include prophetic oracles, history, and poetry. Kings and governments are not the answer to human chaos, so God uses the prophets to confront, instruct, and guide the people of God.

Four hundred years after the last book of the Old Testament, human history is transformed with the emergence of Jesus the Messiah. The four Gospels—Matthew, Mark, Luke, and John—tell the story of Jesus both as personal history and as expressions of faith. They are "gospel," good news. Luke continues the story by telling the dramatic events in the mission of Jesus' designated representatives in the Acts of the apostles. The promise made to Abraham 2,000 years earlier, that through his family "all the nations of the earth would be blessed" is dramatically revealed for the first time as the message about Jesus spreads across empires and continents.

The letters the apostle Paul wrote to Christian communities and individuals and the "general epistles" of the New Testament contain fresh new teachings about life, usually in response to problems. They also reveal the character of God, now viewed from the higher plane of revelation following the pouring out of the Spirit of God.

The book of Revelation both fascinates and puzzles us. Its kaleidoscope of oracles and judgments and images knocks us out of complacency. But Revelation is also a book of comfort. God sets things right. And so things come full circle. From garden to paradise.

This is "the big picture." In it we will find harsh truths and life-giving truths, but only as we read them in the light of the great reality of God.

Chapter 4

WHAT ABOUT BIBLE TRANSLATIONS?

If you are wondering what English translation of the Bible to use, know this: you are blessed with an array of excellent choices. In the past few hundred years, interest in and reverence for the Bible has inspired major efforts involving thousands of researchers, linguists, and translators. The complete Bible is available in about 500 languages today, with thousands more having portions of the Bible in translation.

The purpose of Bible translation is to accurately render the meaning of biblical texts from their original languages—Hebrew and Aramaic for the Old Testament, and Greek for the New Testament—into a "receptor language." Scholars and committees of scholars use the latest knowledge of ancient manuscripts to express accurately what the original authors of Scripture meant.

Why are there dozens of different English translations? It is because there are options as to how Bible translators carry the meaning of Greek and Hebrew texts into the receptor language. For example, some translations aim at rendering the meaning of texts word-for-word (sometimes referred to as "literal" translations). The upside to this approach is that the Bible reader can know the specific word choice and phraseology of the biblical authors. The downside is that Bible texts translated in this way can be more difficult to read. Until one gets used to the style, it can seem stiff, wooden, and unfamiliar—but one can certainly get used to it.

Another approach is to translate thought for thought. Translation done in this way will have language that is more familiar to English readers, and thus probably easier to read. Translating in this way can still be regarded as accurate, if the true meaning of the original text is carried across.

Then there is the method of free translation or paraphrase, the purpose of which is to give readers the flow of the biblical text idea by idea, oftentimes rendering the meaning of whole sentences in new ways, rather than carrying over the exact words of the Hebrew or Greek. A paraphrase may use the word *flashlight* instead of *lamp*, for instance.

Heated debates surround the issue of Bible translation. People who take the Bible seriously want translations that are accurate and faithful to what the writers of Holy Scripture intended to communicate. But the typical Bible reader can be assured that there is not just one accurate translation. In fact, for the serious believer, the best thing is to have and read different translations for devotional reading, but especially in studying the Bible or preparing to teach it.

Keep this in mind: the best Bible translation is going to be the one you will actually read. If you purchase the latest Bible translation but you don't actually read through it, or if it gathers dust on the shelf, that Bible will be of less value to you than one that you consume because you understand it.

I can speak personally about this. As I was growing up, I tried many times to read the standard mainstream Bible I'd been given in church and failed. But when someone put a brand-new paraphrase of the New Testament in my hand when I was 17 years old, I started reading it and could not put it down. My life was changed that early summer. A year later, I started reading one of the most literal translations available. It was hard work, and it took me the better part of a year, but it was beneficial to me at a different level. In the decades that followed, I got used to referring to numerous translations as I prepared teachings and sermons. I have so much respect for the diligent experts who have given us these gifts.

Here are some of the most popular versions of the Bible in English sold today:

New Living Translation—an easy-to-read thought-by-thought translation from Hebrew and Greek

New International Version—a standard translation using universally used English (thus, "International")

King James Version—the classic 1611 translation that is a landmark in English literature, but far removed from contemporary English

New King James Version—a very literal translation, updating the language of the King James Version

English Standard Version—an "essentially literal" update of the widely used Revised Standard Version

Common English Bible—a new translation blending word-for-word and thought-for-thought approaches

New American Standard Bible—widely seen as the most literal translation produced in the 20th century

The Message—a free translation by Eugene Peterson using everyday modern English, idea for idea

Chapter 5

WHAT HELP CAN WE GET SO WE UNDERSTAND THE BIBLE BETTER?

"Do you understand what you are reading?" That was the question Philip the apostle asked a man from Ethiopia who was riding in a chariot on a desert road leading from Jerusalem toward the Mediterranean Sea (Acts 8). The man was the finance minister of Ethiopia, but he had been in Jerusalem for Pentecost and somehow obtained a copy of Isaiah the prophet. The man's answer? "How can I [understand it] unless someone explains it to me?"

Every person who has ever read the Bible has wondered: *Who can I find who will help me understand what I am reading?* Some will go looking for a book or commentary that explains this or that portion of Scripture; far more people simply let their pastors or other teachers do the heavy lifting of Bible interpretation, and they go along with what they hear as long as they trust the person they listen to.

But most believers come to a point of realizing that they need to let the words of Scripture speak to them, without influence from a human interpreter. This is a healthy instinct because God's word really is a gift from God directly to the believer. Great spiritual movements have happened when ordinary believers rediscover the Bible for themselves. On the other hand, we are meant to live in fellowship with other believers, and to learn the meaning of God's word—together.

There must be a balance here: a work of the Spirit of God in the minds and hearts of the believers as they are illumined by the biblical text for themselves, but with appropriate assistance from more mature people, and from experts on the Bible who are archeologists, historians, linguistic experts, etc.

So, assuming that we know we need to read the Bible for ourselves, and enjoy a lifelong process of discovery and enrichment, what outside resources are available to us to help us along the way?

1. *Study Bibles.* One of the most common ways we can find reliable guidance and information is in the pages of a good study Bible. Most of the common Bible translations have a "study Bible" version, which is the biblical text with further explanation via charts, maps, illustrations, and notes. The notes are brief explanations of words, phrases, people, and events. A study Bible may have tens of thousands of notes in total, usually prepared by a variety of Bible experts. There are dozens of different study Bibles in English. Two that are distinguished by broad-based scholarship are *The NIV Study Bible* (Zondervan) and *The ESV Study Bible* (Crossway).

2. *Bible Dictionaries or Encyclopedias.* For much more information than is contained in the notes of a study Bible, use a Bible dictionary (one or two volumes) or a Bible encyclopedia (multiple volumes, with much more detail). Any serious Scripture reader should acquire at least a one-volume Bible dictionary. A good dictionary contains thousands of brief articles, usually updated every few years, on people, places, doctrines, history, geography, archaeology, and more. In a Bible dictionary, you can look up *the book of Acts*, or *John the apostle*, or *Jericho*, or *sanctification*, or *Messiah*, or *mustard seed*, or *Jordan River*, or *Pontius Pilate*, etc. Bible dictionaries include maps, drawings, charts, and illustrations. They are amazing tools. They don't tell you what specific passages mean, but they give you information that you wouldn't be able to get on your own, to help you understand the Bible better.

3. *Bible Commentaries.* On the desert road, Philip knew the man from Ethiopia was reading a very important Messianic prophecy from the book of Isaiah. When asked about the passage, Philip offered an explanation which led, ultimately, to the Ethiopian becoming a believer and asking to be baptized! Bible commentaries are explanations of the biblical text book by book, passage by passage, verse by verse. The experts who write commentaries help us understand where and when biblical books were written, the historical context from which they have come, the possible meanings of the biblical authors, and ways to work out difficult passages. Commentaries are not sermons. They offer exegesis—which means "working out" the meaning of the original authors.

There are some one-volume commentaries on the Bible, but a commentary devoted to just one book of the Bible is much more helpful. But be aware of this: some commentaries are highly technical, getting into great detail about the Hebrew and Greek text, and they are difficult to use unless you know those languages. Other commentaries are much more usable to the average Bible student, getting right to the meaning of the text without losing the forest for the trees. A commentary series I am particularly fond of is *The Bible Speaks Today* (IVP, Series Editors J. A. Motyer and John Stott).

There are other tools to help us understand the Bible: Bible handbooks; online Bibles, which help us quickly find passages; atlases; etc. But the three main tools listed above will generally give us all the help we need when we, like the Ethiopian, say, "How can I understand it unless someone explains?"

Part II

UNDERSTANDING THE OLD TESTAMENT

Chapter 6

HOW SHOULD WE UNDERSTAND
THE STORIES OF THE
OLD TESTAMENT?

When I was a boy, I was given a set of recordings of dramatized Bible stories, and they captivated my attention. They were well-produced audio narrations complete with sound effects like the clanking of swords, rushing waters, roaring lions, chariots, and nails being driven through Jesus' hands. The stories lodged in my head as I listened to the recordings over and over.

It is common in Christian churches for children to be taught the Bible story by story. Then, somehow, we get the idea that as adults we can handle the higher truths we find in places like the epistles of the New Testament. But this is to miss the grand scheme of the Bible. The backbone of the Bible is story or narrative. If we look at the whole sweep of Scripture from Genesis to Revelation, there is one grand story: the creation, the fall of humanity into sin and corruption, God's efforts at redeeming humanity, and the final remaking of all things. This is the metanarrative of the Bible.

That big story is divided into two large narratives: God working through a chosen people (the old covenant), and then, with the coming of Jesus, how God forged a new covenant open to people from every part of the world. Break that down further, and we get to the individual stories of Joseph, of the exodus, of Ruth, of Joshua, of the destruction of Jerusalem, of Daniel in Babylon—and hundreds of others. So how should we understand the narratives of the Old Testament, which constitute almost half of the Old Testament text?

1. We should read individual narratives in their specific contexts, but with the wider narratives in mind. The story of Ruth, for instance, is a rich and poignant story within itself, about struggle, commitment, faith, and redemption. But then we learn that Ruth was the great-grandmother of King David, so she fits into the wider Old Testament picture. More amazing, this woman from Moab is listed in the genealogy of Jesus because of her lineage with David (Matt. 1:5). So the significance of the story of Ruth goes beyond her relatives and the harvesting of grain.

2. We should take Old Testament narratives at face value, reading for the natural sense. The purpose of narrative is to tell us what happened and to help us understand the broad significance of what happened. Not every story has a moral. The account of Joshua leading the Hebrews across the Jordan River means exactly that. We should not assume there is some symbolic meaning to the river, or to Joshua, or to the place where they crossed. It is wrong-headed to impose a symbolic or allegorical meaning on a biblical story. It is misleading and it is arbitrary. It assumes there is a hidden meaning to biblical stories, which leaves the normal Bible reader to ask: "I wonder what I'm missing here?" No, we should assume the biblical writer meant something specific, coherent, and intelligible story by story. This is to read Scripture on its own terms, respecting the intentionality of the biblical authors. Taking Old Testament narratives at face value removes much of the anxiety we might have if we are always looking for some supposed hidden meaning.

3. We should also avoid moralizing or spiritualizing every Old Testament story we read. What, for instance, might be the moral to the story of Jacob deceiving his brother Esau and later his uncle Laban? The text does not condemn what Jacob did, nor does it endorse his actions. The narrative simply tells us what happened. The story of Joshua's battle for the city of Ai does not mean we ought to obliterate our enemies in life. The story of Isaac finding a wife (Gen. 24) does not give us a method of dating. And Moses going into the tabernacle under the cloud of God's glory is not a guideline for how we should pray or worship. These stories have great significance in the wider narrative of Scripture, but we reduce that significance when we go looking for a "moral to the story." However, these stories do illustrate truths or morals that are taught elsewhere in Scripture. That is the best way to read them.

4. *We should learn from the complex lives of the characters of biblical stories.* We could feel a lot of tension over the fact that even the great heroes of faith in the Old Testament had faults and overt transgressions. The narrative usually doesn't come right out and flag what was honorable or despicable behavior. It is assumed we will figure that out based on the parts of Scripture that do teach morality. The Bible is wonderfully honest. The characters in the narratives are all sinners, yet they are part of the historic unfolding of the greatest story of Scripture: the story of God.

5. *We should read through biblical narrative seeing it as the great story of God who is its central character.* The narrative of the Old Testament reveals the Creator of all things as the God of holiness and of love. In the stories we witness the God of holiness for whom right and wrong, good and evil, really do matter. And his love is seen in his patience, forgiveness, guidance, protection, and mercy.

What is true of all great narratives, and especially the narratives of Holy Scripture, is that every time we

44

go through them, we will see something new. A detail here and there. An attitude in one of the characters. A sight, smell, or sound. A silhouette of an attribute of God. And we will see ourselves, not by imposing ourselves on the narrative, but when we recognize a hope we've had or devastation we've experienced. We see our sins, not just the sins of the characters in the story. And we see hope for all of us who would be without hope if not for the mercy of God.

Chapter 7

WHAT IS THE BIG PICTURE OF THE BOOK OF BEGINNINGS?

If someone were to ask you to take as much time as you wanted to answer the question "Who are you?" you would start at the beginning. Your birth, your parents, your hometown, your ethnicity. To fully understand a person, a people, or a place today, you must go back to their beginnings.

That is why the Bible starts with "In the beginning." Generations of believers have found the meaning and purpose of life—including its tragedies and triumphs—by reading Genesis, the book of beginnings. When we read Genesis we should see the larger part of the God-story in it. The book is not merely a sequence of events. It is a theology about God's intention in creating humanity, about the dreadful corruption within humanity, and about God's way of restoring humanity, beginning with one man and one tribe.

"In the beginning God created the heavens and the earth"—in other words, everything. Right there in just a few Hebrew words, *Bereishit bara Elohim et hashamayim ve'et ha'aretz*, we have a specific definition of reality. First, there is a singular God who chose to create. This eliminates the main alternatives: atheism (no god), polytheism (many gods), and pantheism (god is the universe). In many other ancient religions, there is a god who competes with the sun, moon, stars, and sea monsters who also are gods. In contrast, in Genesis God is Creator of all. It sets forth the perspective carried all the way through Scripture, that there are only two categories in the universe: Creator and created. One Almighty God, and everything else.

And there is order in the creation. God speaks it into existence, and then God commands the way life should work. There is thus a harmony and logic in the creation. For this reason we should not see science and the Bible as exclusive of each other. Science is based on being able to predict the way things will be because there is an order and predictability in nature. This is theologically true, and empirically true.

Genesis puts humanity at the apex of creation, whereas in other religions human beings are slaves to the gods. The revolutionary idea that humanity was created "in the image of God" affirms the dignity and value of human beings. The disobedience of the man and the woman and the fall into sin is all the more tragic because it is a fracturing of the image of God. The book of beginnings describes the genesis of sin in human beings as succumbing to the temptation to rise even higher than their noble place, to believe that they know better than the command of God.

So Genesis speaks of multiple beginnings: of the universe, of humanity, of sin, of the nations, and of one nation in particular which God would use to define the right life. Most of the book of Genesis (chapters 12 through 50) tells the story of the patriarchs of Israel: Abraham, Isaac, Jacob, and the sons of Jacob who produced the tribes of the Hebrews numbering hundreds of thousands by the end of the book. This is the people of God. A particular tribe whom God used in particular ways in order to establish universal principles.

In the New Testament, the apostle Paul interprets Genesis as he describes the essence of the meaning of Abraham's story. Grace through faith. Righteousness as right relationship. Patience in the promise. And so on. The truth of Genesis reaches to where we live. Abraham was justified by faith, and thus it always must be (Rom. 4; Gal. 3; Heb. 11).

We see in the narratives about Abraham, Sarah, Isaac, Jacob, Esau, Joseph and his brothers, and many others a raw depiction of human virtue and vice, of faith in God and contention with God. We are not to take their behaviors as prescriptions for what we should do in our lives, and there isn't necessarily a moral to every story. The text does not tell us story by story which actions of these people were right and which were wrong. Genesis gives the narrative, and the whole of Scripture is the magnifying glass through which we examine it.

We need to read Genesis in context so we'll get the whole sweeping truth of it. Occasionally it is beneficial to read Genesis all the way through in three or four sittings, looking for the big themes. When we do so, we'll see in it the greatness of God, the dignity and tragedy of humanity, and the piecemeal, plodding process whereby one tribe learns lessons for all of us. Genesis sets the tone of everything else in Scripture. It contains the DNA of the people of God.

So if someone asks you to take as much time as you want to say who you are, you might consider starting with Genesis.

Chapter 8

HOW SHOULD WE
UNDERSTAND THE LAW?

Most people who start to read the Bible from the beginning for the first time will typically have this experience: Genesis is fascinating with the story of creation, Babel, the flood, and the epic stories of Abraham, Isaac, and Jacob. The exodus story is gripping. And then comes the law. Mount Sinai and the Ten Commandments are familiar. Next come the flurry of laws and stipulations, many of which are so far removed from our culture and hard to understand that the Bible reader can get bogged down. Mid-Leviticus, typically.

What is "the law"? What is the purpose of the more than 600 regulations? And, very importantly, how much of this applies to our lives? Why do we believe that "You shall not commit adultery" in the Ten Commandments applies to us but "Do not wear clothing woven of two kinds of material" does not?

In Scripture "the law" may refer to the more than 600 regulations Moses passed on to the people in Exodus, Leviticus, Numbers, and Deuteronomy, or it may refer to the first five books of the Bible, or as shorthand for the entire pattern of religious life and rituals in the Old Testament. Law is a way for any society to define the proper bounds of behavior both for protection and for flourishing. But the law of the Old Testament is unique in that it was God's way of shaping his relationship with a covenant people.

This will help us understand the sometimes bewildering array of laws, some of which seem strange to us. The Hebrews were chosen to live in a distinctive way by how they dressed, what they ate, and how they worshipped. Most of these laws do not carry over after the coming of Christ, when the old covenant gave way to the new covenant, and the way of living in obedience to God comes via a higher kind of law.

In Exodus through Deuteronomy there are three kinds of laws. First, there are *civil regulations*, for instance, property rights; marriage and divorce standards; laws sanctioning theft, murder, and other crimes; health regulations; etc. Then there are *ritual instructions* that define the sacrificial system, the festivals, the role of the Levites, and the specific physical features of the tabernacle. Finally, there are *moral princi-*

ples, which include sexual ethics, the major themes of the Ten Commandments, and more. These three types are sometimes called the civil law, the ceremonial law, and the moral law.

So how do we know which of the 600 laws in the Old Testament apply to Christians today? Should we avoid eating shellfish? Ought we to observe Passover? Is it wrong to steal? Do we have to observe the Sabbath (i.e., rest on the seventh day of the week, Saturday)? Are sexual relations between blood relatives wrong? Is tithing (i.e., giving 10 percent of your income) an eternal commandment?

We have to answer this question on something better than our intuitions. The terms of the new covenant must guide us here, and what we find in the New Testament is that the civil law was God's way of shaping Hebrew society; it's not binding today. The ritual law used sacrifice and festivals and the tabernacle to teach lessons about sin and atonement, but it has now been superseded by the work of Christ. (See the teaching in the New Testament book of Hebrews.) Moral laws have ongoing validity, but mostly because they are repeated in one form or another in the New Testament.

But lest we repeat the legalism and self-righteousness of the Pharisees and teachers of the law of Jesus' day, we are guided in the new covenant by this one transcendent principle: the law of love or "the law of Christ" (Gal. 6:2). Jesus said the whole old covenant law can be summed up by "Love the Lord your God with all your heart and with all your soul and with all your mind" and "Love your neighbor as yourself" (Matt. 22:37-40). Paul put it this way: "the entire law is fulfilled in keeping this one command: 'Love your neighbor as yourself'" (Gal. 5:14), and "love is the fulfillment of the law" (Rom. 13:8-10).

It would be reasonable to ask: "So if most of the Law in the first five books of the Bible does not apply to us today, in what sense is it part of the word of God for us?" Here is where we need to set aside all self-centeredness. The whole sweep of the biblical narrative is the story of God moving among and within people in order to bring salvation to humanity, but that doesn't mean every verse is about us. The law of the Old Testament is the word of God for all people for all time, but given to specific people groups in the context of God's dynamic, upward development of a covenant relationship with human beings. The apostle Paul puts it this way: "The law was our guardian [custodian, tutor] until Christ came that we might be justified by faith" (Gal. 3:24).

So the law stands as a true expression of the will and the ways of God, expressed in a particular era, subject to modification, providing the basis for ever higher revelations of what it means to be the covenant people of God. Jesus summed it up when he said: "I have not come to abolish [the Law or the Prophets] but to fulfill them" (Matt. 5:17).

Chapter 9

WHAT IS IMPORTANT ABOUT
THE LAND OF THE BIBLE?

One of the ways we know that the truth of the Bible is rooted in reality is that the story of the Bible—the drama of God's interaction with humanity—unfolds in a real place. This is a real God engaging with real people across a timeline that goes for thousands of years in a specific part of the world. The Bible is not detached philosophy. It tells us what *happened* (in history) so that we can understand what *happens* (in life).

After the Pentateuch (the first five books of Scripture), there is a major transition as the wandering Israelites entered the ancient land of Canaan. Under Joshua, the Israelite armies conquered this territory promised to them by God as an inheritance (Josh. 1:1-6). The small land of Israel, just 200 miles long and

100 miles wide, would be the main stage for the drama of redemption until the world-changing mission of the apostles—altogether a span of two millennia.

What is it like, this "good and spacious land, a land flowing with milk and honey" (Ex. 3:8)? To the Hebrews who had left slavery in Egypt 40 years earlier, it was a true blessing. It wasn't paradise, but the plains and hills were a good land for farmers who grew crops of wheat and barley, who developed groves of olive and fig trees, and tended vineyards. The coastal climate is similar to that of Southern California.

In the Old Testament, we find the connecting points between land, life, and theology. The three great festivals (Passover, Firstfruits, and Ingathering) corresponded to the beginning and end of harvests. Rain is the grace of God. Food on the table is the blessing of God. Drought is a time of testing. The land also supported the herding of sheep and goats. So it was easy to describe God's care as his shepherding (Ps. 23), and Jesus as "the good shepherd." Real land, real life, real people, real God.

But Israel was a difficult land to live in from a political point of view. The surrounding kingdoms were an almost continual threat, and part of that has to do with the geography of the land of Israel. If you look at a map of the region, what you will see is that this small strip of land is hemmed in by the Mediterranean Sea to the west and the Arabian Desert to the east. Then, to make things even more complicated, the region to the north and east—known as Mesopotamia—was home to a succession of aggressive empires: Assyria, Babylonia, Persia. To the south and west of Israel lay the great land of Egypt. So Israel is a small bridge of land between sea and desert, standing in the way of superpowers to the northeast and the southwest. This explains much of the history of the Old Testament. It is amazing, actually, that there were even brief times when Israel was strong enough to have security and stability.

To understand more about this place and the events that transpired there, picture this bird's-eye view of the land. Going across the land from west to east, there are five main regions (picture them like strips running north to south). First, is the coastal plain. Flat, fertile, and lush, this is a desirable part of the land, and thus contested by people like the Philistines who occupied the southern coast for centuries. Chariot battles happened here—not so in the central mountainous region of the land.

To the east of the coastal plain are the foothills known as the Shephelah, which slope upwards to about 1,300 feet. The gentle hills of this region are also fertile, crisscrossed with olive groves and fig trees. It is also the battleground for many fights in the eras of Joshua and the Judges, and it's the region where David famously stood up to the Philistine champion Goliath.

Moving east again, we come to the central mountainous region including Judea and Samaria. These low mountains—rising to just 3,500 feet—are rocky limestone hills, undulating across the landscape. Jerusalem sits on a set of such hills, as does Bethlehem.

The fourth region is the Jordan River Valley, which drops dramatically from the central mountains to below sea level.

And finally, to the east again, the high plateau region known as Transjordan rises. From here Moses viewed the Promised Land he was not allowed to enter.

In the north is the fertile plain and productive sea known as Galilee. More about that when we get to the New Testament.

This is "the land." More than geography or a patch on a map, it is central to the covenant promise of God. Yet by the time we get to the new covenant, we find that God's geography and the mission of his people extends to the whole world, just as he promised to Abraham, the man from Mesopotamia who walked across the chalky hills—"all peoples on earth will be blessed through you" (Gen. 12:3).

Chapter 10

HOW SHOULD WE INTERPRET WHAT THE PROPHETS HAD TO SAY?

It's okay to be honest if you're having difficulty understanding sections of the Bible. Remember, our difficulty understanding Scripture is not a problem. It is what you'd expect of a body of scriptures that speak into the complexities of human experience, and contain the high truth of a transcendent God. When we come to the Prophets, typically the questions that get asked are: *What are they talking about? Is this about them or us? Is prophecy about the past or the future?*

Remember that when you're interpreting the Bible, the simplest and most natural explanation is always best. When Jeremiah speaks about Babylon, he means Babylon. Amos was really warning about the armies of the Assyrians descending on Israel. Haggai's words about the rebuilding of the temple were about events during that period when the Jews were allowed to return to Jerusalem. Most of the events the Old Testament prophets spoke about were fulfilled in the era in which they were spoken. What we get to do all these centuries later is pull out and apply these truths and principles, and apply them in fresh ways in our lives.

In the Old Testament, the prophet was a person who was called to bring the word of God to the people. The prophet was not a fortune-teller or soothsayer. He was not reporting the headlines of the news, mysteriously, before they were written. The prophet was a proclaimer. He brought words of assurance and promise, as well as confrontation and warning. Many people are called prophets: Abraham, Moses, Elijah, Elisha, etc., whose prophetic activity (i.e., being God's representative to the people) is embedded in the historical narratives.

There are 16 Old Testament books we call "the Prophets." Four "Major Prophets": Isaiah, Jeremiah, Ezekiel, Daniel; and the so-called "Minor Prophets": Amos through Malachi. ("Major" and "Minor" only mean their length, not their importance.) All of these books were written within a narrow 300-year span, from 760 to 460 B.C. This helps us understand their purpose. All the prophetic books of the Old Testament were God's word to his covenant people, warning them and bolstering them during periods of pronounced spiritual and national danger.

The honest truth of the Bible is that men and women—even those blessed to be the covenant people of God—kept falling into sin. It is sobering to read through the Old Testament and encounter never-ending cycles of obedience and disobedience. So God spoke through the prophets. They confronted, warned, and assured. They did offer predictions, most typically showing the cause and effect of disobedience and unfaithfulness. Every oracle of every prophet means something specific. The challenge is that most of us do not have an encyclopedic knowledge of Tyre and Sidon, of Persia, of Darius, of the Nazirites, of Ekron, and of Meshek and Tubal.

Some passages in the Prophets clearly point to events to be fulfilled centuries later, for instance predictions of the coming Messiah. Isaiah 53 is widely understood to be pointing to Jesus. "He was despised and rejected by mankind, a man of suffering, and familiar with pain" (v. 3).

Then there are some passages that appear to be fulfilled in the era of the prophet, but also extend out to the Messianic Age or the end of time. It is possible for a prophecy to have multiple fulfillments, though we have to make sure this is clearly called for in the passage.

So here are some recommendations on reading the Prophets:

1. *Read these books naturally and in ample segments, not verse by verse.* Listen for the spiritual movement within prophetic oracles, rather than getting bogged down in details. Catch the big-picture spiritual dynamics and message of the oracles. For instance, the disposition of God (e.g., disappointed, indignant, sorrowful, tender, caring), the condition of the people addressed (e.g., frightened, disobedient, humbled, arrogant), the predictions of what might or will happen (e.g., captivity, deliverance, famine, restoration). The best thing we gain from the prophetic books is not about events on timelines, but the great spiritual realities of life, including insights into disobedience and sin, and the judgment and mercy of God.

2. *Use Bible helps.* In reading the Prophets, we will benefit greatly from good Bible dictionaries and commentaries. Look for commentaries where the original setting and meaning of the Prophets are respected and explained. Unfortunately, there are many commentators, preachers, and teachers who assume prophecy is mostly about events yet to unfold in our day, when the biblical text indicates otherwise. This is crystal ball interpretation. It is arbitrary, misleading, and does not respect the call of the Prophets. It overlooks the plain meaning of the biblical text, which must be our first priority.

3. *Go ahead and apply the spiritual lessons of the Prophets to life today.* These 16 Old Testament books are the word of God to us, as long as we allow for the different terms of the old covenant and what we stand on today, the new covenant.

4. *Be enriched by the word of the Prophets.* Don't be discouraged by their complexity or sometimes-dire message. It is only because God loves humanity that he spoke through the prophets—hard truth included.

Chapter 11

HOW SHOULD WE
READ THE PSALMS?

The Bible is not just a book. It is relationship in words. God's word to men and women, boys and girls. A living action between the almighty Creator of the universe and his most cherished creation: humanity. We do not understand Scripture unless we hear in it the divine-human dialogue.

The Psalms prove this. In the beloved 150 songs and poems in the middle of the Bible, we witness not just God speaking to us, but the privilege we have of speaking to God. This is the essence of relationship: two parties interacting with each other. And what an interaction! The Psalms express the full range of states of the human heart:

Thanksgiving and praise... "Give thanks to the LORD, for he is good; his love endures forever" (Ps. 107:1).

Lament... "My God, my God, why have you forsaken me? Why are you so far from saving me, so far from my cries of anguish?" (Ps. 22:1).

Celebration... "I lift up my eyes to you, to you who sit enthroned in heaven" (Ps. 123:1).

Wisdom... "Unless the LORD builds the house, the builders labor in vain. Unless the LORD watches over the city, the guards stand watch in vain" (Ps. 127:1).

Judgment... "Pour out your wrath on them; let your fierce anger overtake them. May their place be deserted; let there be no one to dwell in their tents" (Ps. 69:24-25).

In the Psalms we find honest, sometimes brutal, expressions of the human heart. The Bible would not be valuable if it were a string of sentimental platitudes or religious propaganda. But it is not. The songs and poems that are the Psalms express the highest joy and the deepest sorrow. Their authors plead with God, shout at God, beg God for forgiveness. They exalt virtues and righteousness, and they condemn in the bitterest terms the ugly abuses people sometimes carry out. The Psalms teach about the attributes of God ("the LORD is my Shepherd," 23:1) and the history of God ("[he] swept Pharaoh and his army into the Red Sea," 136:15). They speak of humanity's great potential ("You have made them a little lower than the angels and crowned them with glory and honor," 8:5) and the darkness of human depravity ("shame will come on those who are treacherous without cause," 25:3).

So how should we read this "treasury," as Charles Spurgeon called it? First, some facts. The Psalms were the songs written to be used by the Israelites in their worship life—both personal and communal. The titles on the Psalms indicate that almost half of them were "of David," and some others are identified as being written by various composers—"sons of Asaph," "sons of Korah," Solomon, Moses. They were made into a collection after the Jews returned from exile.

The many quotations from the Psalms that appear in the New Testament reveal that these songs were deeply embedded in the minds and hearts of the Jews. Most people today love the Psalms, and whether they realize it or not, the poetry has much to do with it. After all, one could state the proposition: "God is timeless, but people come and go." Or one could paint with words, which is what Psalm 90 does:

A thousand years in your sight
  are like a day that has just gone by,
  or like a watch in the night.
Yet you sweep people away in the sleep of death—
  they are like the new grass of the morning:
In the morning it springs up new,
  but by evening it is dry and withered. (vv. 4-6)

The Psalms are the most sensory part of God's word, including this delicious invitation:

Taste and see that the LORD is good;
  blessed is the one who takes refuge in him.
  (Ps. 34:8)

So how should we read the Psalms with understanding? For one thing, we should read slowly and deliberately in order to take in the sights and sounds, taste, touch and smell in which the truth of God is contained. Try reading a Psalm a day aloud—which is how all people in the ancient world read. For millennia people have meditated on the Psalms, storing up their treasures, frequently to be recalled during critical times of life.

We should also pray the Psalms. Let the voice of the Psalm you are reading be your voice, even if your life circumstance is not the same of the particular Psalm you are reading. Put yourself in the shoes of the writer, and you will understand the realities in the Psalm. For example, sense the pathos in Psalm 137, composed in the exile:

> By the rivers of Babylon we sat and wept
>> when we remembered Zion.
> There on the poplars
>> we hung our harps,
> for there our captors asked us for songs. (vv. 1-3a)

This should put a lump in our throats.

Do not look down at the Psalms with a magnifying glass. Pray them upwards with a megaphone. The word *heart* appears 131 times in this book of the Bible, which seems only appropriate since in the Psalms we have the heart of humanity reaching out to the heart of God.

What a privilege to have this pathway to God.

Chapter 12

WHAT SHOULD WE TAKE FROM THE BOOKS OF WISDOM (PROVERBS, ECCLESIASTES, JOB)?

If you were to stumble upon a long-lost manuscript that no eyes had seen for generations, and if you were to read its opening lines which offered a "wisdom" like what's described in the following lines, you might consider it one of the greatest discoveries of your life.

> Proverbs... for gaining wisdom and instruction;
> for understanding words of insight;
> for receiving instruction in prudent behavior,
> doing what is right and just and fair;
> for giving prudence to those who are simple,
> knowledge and discretion to the young—
> let the wise listen and add to their learning,

and let the discerning get guidance. (Ps. 1:1-5)

These are the opening lines of the book of Proverbs, one of three books in the Old Testament (Proverbs, Job, and Ecclesiastes) called "wisdom literature" (although other books contain sections of a similar kind). So, in addition to historical narrative, law, prophecy, and poetry, the Bible also has this lively, deep, and profound set of books referred to as "wisdom." These are books about real life.

Proverbs is a book of practical wisdom. Job is an epic story exploring the deep issues of suffering, purpose, and God. Ecclesiastes offers a sharp-edged perspective on the hard realities of life. Once again, we see the utter honesty of the Scriptures. We see the disordered state of the world and human nature, and guidance on seeking the order of God.

Any believer would do well to read the book of Proverbs once a year, if not more often. These Hebrew proverbs (*meshalim*) are short, pithy statements of truth and practical guidance. They address life issues like attitude and speech, sexuality, poverty and prosperity, marriage and family issues, and much more. The statements are brief, vivid, and memorable. Because of this style, they include figures of speech, so we must understand the main point of the statement.

For instance: "Honor the LORD with your wealth, with the firstfruits of all your crops; then your barns will be filled to overflowing, and your vats will brim over with new wine" (3:9-10). You may not be a farmer who owns barns and vineyards, but you can still get the big point: Honor God with all that you own, making giving a top priority, and you will do well in life.

When you read the Proverbs, always keep in mind that *they are general statements of what is generally true.* The writer does not claim they are promises from God or guarantees of what *always* happens. The original readers did not assume that if you honored God by giving the firstfruits of your crops, the barns would always and forever overflow. Droughts happen. Barns burn down. Thieves prowl. Life happens. But the principle is *generally* and *typically* true.

Many parents have counted on Proverbs 22:6, which says, "Train up a child in the way he should go; even when he is old he will not depart from it" (ESV). Therefore, some are bewildered when their grown-up children do "depart" from lives of virtue and health. They may be left thinking, *We must not have done the training part right.* But the proverb is not a guarantee. It is guidance—true, helpful, and clear. Parents should take the moral development of their children seriously; and most of the time, those planted seeds will bear fruit. But not every time.

The book of Proverbs is good as gold as a divinely inspired guidebook for right living. It confronts us about sloth and anger and theft and lewdness and gossip. It guides us toward prosperity through prudence, and contentment through simplicity.

It is important to *read the book of Proverbs in sections, rather than one verse at a time.* Selecting a single verse out of context will lead to misunderstanding and prevent us from seeing the whole. We must look at the painting, not the brushstrokes. As in reading the Psalms, let the power of the images hit home. And when you do find a single statement that could be a landmark verse for you, go ahead and memorize it (as long as you understand it in context). "Trust in the Lord with all your heart and lean not on your own understanding; in all your ways submit to him, and he will make your paths straight" (3:5-6).

Finally, just a word about two other Old Testament books that are unique. The book of Job contains wisdom, but embedded in it is the heart-rending story of a man undergoing unbelievable suffering. The main characters in the drama say many things that aren't true at all; for instance, all suffering is the direct result of specific sins and failings. But in the end, Job finds solace in God himself and not philosophical answers.

To some people, the book of Ecclesiastes reads like a statement of hopelessness. Rather, it is a brutally honest description of the dark side of life, which ought to propel us onto the mercy of God.

Chapter 13

WHAT IS IMPORTANT ABOUT
THE ERA OF THE KINGS?

I remember when I first read the Old Testament books that recount the stories of the kings of Israel and Judah. David's and Solomon's reigns are epic. But then begins the long and oftentimes sordid story of about 40 successive kings, most of whom were "evil." I remember thinking: *This is hardly encouraging reading!* Yet buried in the history is the story of God, and we must understand it.

In the middle of the story of the Old Testament is an era spanning five centuries in which we hear about the checkered history of the kings of Judah and Israel, the high points and low points of the people of God, and many lessons about integrity and faithfulness, sin and destruction. This is the era of the kings, a complicated narrative that is an important part of the word of God because it is describes the crooked pathway that eventually led to the coming of the Messiah.

The era of the kings began with the people saying it wasn't enough for God to be their king—they wanted a man to rule them, just like all the other nations. They did indeed become like all the other nations—but not for the good.

The era of the kings stretches from the reign of Saul, a thousand years before Christ, to the destruction of Judah and the exile of the last king in 586 B.C.

Before there was a king, the Israelite tribes lived in scattered, small settlements with judges like Gideon, Deborah, and Jephthah providing a degree of leadership. Then the period of the kings, as told in the books of 1 and 2 Samuel, 1 and 2 Kings, and 1 and 2 Chronicles, is divided into two parts. The first three kings—Saul, David, and Solomon—spanned more than 100 years in what is sometimes called the "golden age" or "the united monarchy." After Solomon there was civil war, and the 12 tribes of Israel divided themselves into a northern kingdom, called "Israel," which included 10 of the tribes, and a southern kingdom made up of the remaining two tribes, called "Judah."

After the disappointing narrative of the reign of Saul, the mostly optimistic accounts of the golden era under David and his son Solomon describe Israel as a rapidly expanding empire that eventually enjoyed a period of peace and stability. David established Jerusalem as the capital, and the center point of the spiritual life of the nation. Solomon advanced that with the building of the temple.

But faithfulness to God is a fragile thing. After Solomon's reign, civil war split the kingdom in two, and for hundreds of years the bitter fruit of unfaithfulness shaped life in Israel and Judah. As we read the books of Kings and 2 Chronicles, we are struck with almost monotonous patterns: bad kings, good kings who become bad kings, a few good kings who kept their integrity and even introduced reform and revival to the people.

We also learn about the spiritual dynamics behind these movements. Those kings who "did evil in the sight of the LORD" and brought bad times on the people were guilty of the worship of foreign gods, of sacrificing outside the rules defined in the law, and sometimes of stooping to the low level of the foreign religions, including human sacrifice. Whole generations lived in complete violation of the Ten Commandments. They forgot their heritage and their God, and they didn't even know there were Scriptures that had defined them as a people.

So the stories of revival and reform under kings like Hezekiah and Josiah are like sunbursts breaking through a heavy overcast sky. Josiah smashed the sites of idolatrous worship and removed the illegal shrines and priests, mediums, and spiritists. He removed pagan statues that previous kings had put at the entrance to the temple, of all places. And he reinstituted the celebration of Passover for all the people of Judah, which had been neglected for centuries.

Here is the sum of it:

Neither before nor after Josiah was there a king like him who turned to the LORD as he did—with all his heart and with all his soul and with all his strength, in accordance with all the Law of Moses. (2 Kings 23:25)

And in this narrative we have one more proof of the power of the word of God in Holy Scripture: Josiah's revival began after his officials discovered the long-lost and forgotten Book of the Law while carrying out Josiah's orders to repair the temple of the Lord. This was the turning point. When Josiah heard the words read to him, everything suddenly made sense. Generations of corruption. Spiritual confusion. Aimlessness. Josiah tore his robes in repentance. This is one more example of the power of the written word to release people from longstanding spiritual paralysis. It is a lesson for us.

So how should we understand the era of the kings? We must read these books as history, but not just political history. These narratives show us spiritual movements downward and upward. Most of the prophets fit into this story by interpreting how God's people could sink low, but also where there was restoration.

We must not artificially lift verses out of context and claim them as our own. These are the stories of real people in a real place. History does offer lessons. History tells us what happened in the past so we can understand what happens in our world, because human nature remains a constant, for good and for ill.

Chapter 14

WHAT DO WE LEARN FROM THE EXILE AND THE RETURN?

The grand narrative of Scripture speaks to the most urgent needs all people have, including the needs to be connected and grounded, to be protected and to belong, to know who you are and where you fit in. The Bible contains the stories of the people of God when they lost all of that. People torn away from their land, torn up as a people, and torn down by humiliating loss. This is the meaning of the exile in the last sections of the Old Testament in which Israel in the north is destroyed by the Assyrian empire, and Judah in the south is taken into exile by the Babylonians.

It is a heart-rending and poignant part of the old covenant narrative. Remember that the land which the two kingdoms of Israel and Judah occupied is located

precariously between the various empires of Mesopotamia to the northeast (Assyria, Babylonia, Persia), and
Egypt to the southwest. The ruthless Assyrians waged
war with Israel in the north, defeating the tribes in 722
B.C. Prophetic warnings about the Assyrian raids were
sounded loudly and clearly by the prophets Amos,
Hosea, Joel, Isaiah, and others. The Assyrians resettled
their captured lands with other people groups, result-
ing in a mixed population. This is where we get the
Samaritans in the New Testament.

The Babylonian empire under Nebuchadnezzar
assaulted Judah in the south. This is when the unthinkable happened. Jerusalem, the City of David, Zion, the
site of the temple, was put under siege in 597 B.C. The
walls were eventually breached, and the Babylonian
army took all of the educated and skilled members of
the community into exile, hundreds of miles away, into
Babylon. The prophet Ezekiel was among them.

But even though God's people were displaced from
their land, their homes, and their temple, God was still
present with them: "While I was among the exiles by
the Kebar River, the heavens were opened and I saw
visions of God" (Ezek. 1:1). And what visions they
were! Four fantastic living creatures, chariot-like
wheels covered in eyes careening through the sky, a
valley of dry bones, and on and on. The prophets Jeremiah, Habakkuk, and Ezekiel also spoke about the im-
pending exile.

I remember when I first read these parts of the Old Testament thinking I had no clue how to understand them. There were people and places and images that were a bit familiar to me, but the big question was how to put it all together. I also remember being put off by teachers, authors, and preachers who seemed to be connecting details of the oracles of the prophets with events in my own time in an arbitrary way. They seemed to be reading Ezekiel as if it were written just about us, and their interpretations seemed stretched, to say the least.

Remember, the meaning of the text of Scripture for us is grounded in what it meant for its original audience. So the prophetic predictions of war and exile and eventual return are primarily about the real history of God's people six and seven centuries before Jesus. It is a compelling story, full of insight about human nature and the nature of this world, which we must apply fully to our lives today. But we must use all means to understand what these oracles meant back then. Here is where excellent commentaries and Bible dictionaries and encyclopedias are indispensable. We must still read these late texts of the Old Testament in an uncluttered and unfiltered manner, letting all the images and pronouncements impact us. But then we ought to avail ourselves of the best tools to understand the details.

The exile is tragedy, but it is matched by the hopeful story of the return of God's people to the land described in Ezra and Nehemiah, and in the last three books of the Old Testament, the prophets Haggai, Zechariah, and Malachi. Even before the destruction of Israel and the exile of Judah happened, the prophets spoke of eventual restoration.

Indeed, some 70 years after Jerusalem was emptied and the temple was destroyed, the leader of a new dominant empire, Cyrus of Persia, decreed that Jews be allowed to return to their land and begin a process of reconstruction. The book of Nehemiah documents reconstruction of the city; the book of Ezra, the reconstruction of the spiritual life of the people. This is different from most history. In the story of the return of the Jews, we see the central importance of worship as the people begin sacrificing again on the site of the old temple, the importance of the word of God as Ezra reads the book of the Law in the hearing of all the people, the importance of moral leadership.

We also see in the return the unchanging covenant of God, the central theme of the Old Testament. Through Ezra and others, the people rediscover the Book of God, and through it they remember the God of creation, of the covenant with Abram, of the deliverance in the exodus, of the land. And all of this in spite of the disobedience and unfaithfulness of the people. This is God then, and God now.

Part III

UNDERSTANDING THE NEW TESTAMENT

Chapter 15

WHAT SHOULD WE UNDERSTAND ABOUT THE WORLD OF THE NEW TESTAMENT?

When we turn the page from Malachi to Matthew, from the Old Testament to the New Testament, from Ezra the scribe and Haggai the prophet to John the Baptist and Jesus of Nazareth, we enter an entirely different world—and we must understand it. The gap between the testaments, known as the intertestamental period, is 400 years, but what happened during those centuries set the stage upon which everything in the life of Jesus and the expansive mission of his followers would take place.

Galatians 4:4-5 says: "When the set time had fully come, God sent his Son, born of a woman, born under the law, to redeem those under the law, that we might receive adoption to sonship." Other translations use the phrase "in the fullness of time." We're told that the life of Jesus, the coming of Messiah, occurred just when God intended. And what a time it was.

Read just a few chapters in one of the Gospels and you'll encounter Romans and Herodians, Jews and Gentiles, Pharisees and Sadducees, teachers of the law and ordinary country folk, and many others. We need to understand who these people were in order to understand the role they played in the great drama that is the New Testament. Turning to a good one-volume Bible dictionary is an excellent way to quickly look up a name, a group, a movement, a place, or anything else. Reading one article on "The Pharisees" will greatly help you understand the Gospels.

The world of the New Testament includes the land of Israel, of course, but the book of Acts and the letters of Paul launch us out into the wider Greco-Roman world surrounding the Mediterranean Sea. Jesus' entire life and ministry took place in the tight geographical stretch from the hills of Judea to the fertile plains and lakeside villages of Galilee. When he was in Jerusalem, Jesus had tense encounters with Jewish religious officials and Roman authorities. When he was in Galilee, near his hometown, his interactions were with ordinary people. The apostle Paul, on the other hand, traveled by boat and caravan and on foot into Syria, Asia

Minor, Crete, Greece, and Italy. The epic story of his life included chains, prison, and trials in front of magistrates that turned into sermons.

The world of the New Testament was a clashing and blending of Jewish, Greek, and Roman cultures.

The exiles who returned from captivity in Babylonia in the days of Ezra and Nehemiah gradually rebuilt Judea, a much smaller entity than what Israel was at its zenith. In 330 B.C., 200 years after the start of the return, Alexander the Great rolled across Judea with his formidable army and began a long and decisive domination of the Jews. Greek (or Hellenistic) culture was hard to resist. The Greek language was dominant, and that is why all the books of the New Testament were originally written in Greek. More than two centuries before Jesus' birth, the Old Testament had been translated into Greek (the Septuagint). This "Greek Old Testament" was used by many of the New Testament authors and of generations of Christians thereafter who did not know a bit of Hebrew.

Alexander's successors split his empire, and the division known as the Seleucids were the next power to dominate Judea. One of their kings, Antiochus Epiphanes (who reigned from 175–164 B.C.), decided to defile the temple of the Jews and to establish an idolatrous religion there. This outrage led eventually to a heroic Jewish revolt under the Maccabees, and eventually Jewish independence that lasted for about 100 years, starting in 166 B.C.

Then came the Romans. General Pompey conquered Jerusalem in 63 B.C., and in 37 B.C. Herod the Great was made king of the Jews by the Roman Senate. But the Romans dominated Judea, occupying it with its army and taxing everyone they could. In the Gospel accounts, many times Jesus' detractors tried to get him to make politically risky comments, as when they asked him whether it was right to pay taxes to Caesar. Most people who were looking for the Messiah were expecting a strong leader who would repel the Romans from Judea.

In the world of the New Testament, particularly the Gospels, we run into two important religious sects or orders, the Pharisees and Sadducees. These were social movements going back to the days of Jewish independence a century and a half before Jesus. Their original purpose was noble: to preserve Jewish identity, including its spiritual integrity, by faithful obedience to the law and the rites. By the time of Jesus, however, far too many Pharisees had become misshapen by the diseases of self-righteousness, legalism, and spiritual blindness.

"When the set time had fully come, God sent his Son" (Gal. 4:4a). The world of the New Testament is a varied and confusing mass of religions, philosophies, political parties, religious groups, and ethnicities.

There were many gods in the Greco-Roman world; but, as always, people were waiting for a truth that rose above all of that—which is exactly what they found in the gospel of Jesus.

Chapter 16

WHAT ARE THE GOSPELS?

Believers do not sit passively waiting to hear the voice of God. They long to hear it. They believe God has not left humanity in silence, but has spoken loudly and clearly through "the Word" that is Holy Scripture and "the Word" that is Jesus the Christ. The opening words of the book of Hebrews confirms that this is true:

> In the past God spoke to our ancestors through the prophets at many times and in various ways, but in these last days he has spoken to us by his Son, whom he appointed heir of all things, and through whom also he made the universe. The Son is the radiance of God's glory and the exact representation of his being, sustaining all things by his power-

ful word. After he had provided purification for sins, he sat down at the right hand of the Majesty in heaven. (Heb. 1:1-3)

This is the big picture. God did not leave humanity in desperate silence. He spoke through men called prophets, and then he decisively spoke to humanity through his Son, Jesus the Messiah. Jesus is not just the word of God, but is also the embodiment of God's glory and very being. Jesus the Christ is the central theme of all of Scripture because his life, death, and resurrection provided a way of redemption.

Jesus takes the stage in the four biblical documents called "the Gospels." Nothing could be more important in our reading of Scripture than understanding the meaning and message of Matthew, Mark, Luke, and John. It would be easy to think these books are historical narratives because they tell the events of Jesus' life. But they are more than that. The Gospels are also more than biography—the telling of one person's story. The Gospels are a unique kind of literature because their purpose is to proclaim the truth that the Son of God appeared in Judea and Galilee, was authenticated by great miracles, was killed, and rose from death in final victory over sin, Satan, and death itself.

The Gospels are proclamation. Their authors are evangelists. So they do not read like modern historical accounts. Their authors were true believers, not just historians. Given the emphasis on truth in their writings, they can be taken as honest and truthful witnesses.

The first time I read through the New Testament, I remember being somewhat puzzled about why there are four Gospels. The simple answer is that four different people had their own reasons to write the true story of Jesus. Mark's Gospel was written first, and much of his content appears in Matthew and Luke. Matthew tells more of the story and has a special interest in explaining the story of Jesus to first-century Jews. Luke, on the other hand, is trying to help a Gentile audience, and he says right at the start that he wants to offer "an orderly account" in order to bolster certainty in the faith.

John's Gospel includes many actions not reported in the other Gospels. It also includes more of Jesus' teaching, much of it in long discourses. The opening prologue of the Gospel gives a cosmic perspective:

In the beginning was the Word, and the Word was with God, and the Word was God. He was with God in the beginning. Through him all things were made; without him nothing was made that has been made. In him was life, and that life was the light of all mankind (John 1:1-4).

New Testament scholar Leon Morris said the Gospel of John is shallow enough for a child to wade in, yet deep enough for an elephant to swim in. All the Gospels, not just John, require deep reflection and study over a lifetime to appreciate their meaning. Be careful if you think you understand "I am the way and the truth and the life" (John 14:6), or "Whoever does not take up their cross and follow me is not worthy of me" (Matt. 10:38), or "your kingdom come, your will be done" (Matt. 6:10). We may understand at one level, but the impact of the sayings of Jesus will always have greater impact on us the longer we study them. They take a lifetime to comprehend and apply. The greatness and the grace of Jesus' teachings expand toward every horizon of life.

One last point: It is very easy to read the words of Jesus as if he were speaking directly to us, yet there is some risk in doing that. His teaching certainly is for us, and its meaning will transform our lives. But we still need to understand his teaching in its original context, as the Jewish Messiah speaking to his varied audience—disciples, followers, the curious, and enemies. And then we can explore how his truth applies to us.

Chapter 17

HOW SHOULD WE UNDERSTAND THE TEACHINGS OF JESUS?

If someone asked you who your favorite teacher was when you were growing up, chances are someone specific would come to mind. And chances are you still respect that person today not because he or she was a fantastic lecturer, or had a superior knowledge of the subject matter, or had a memorable voice. Our favorite teachers—the ones who influenced not just our thinking, but our lives—are usually those people who taught us about life. And it wasn't just with their words. Their own lives were distinctive.

Jesus is widely considered the greatest teacher of all time. But we will only understand him in this capacity if we consider setting and context. Jesus was not a college lecturer or a mystical philosopher. Those who were under the teaching of Jesus were following him on foot, from one village to the next. They heard a parable when he walked into a field of grain, a discourse on being the bread sent from heaven after he fed a multitude, and debriefings with his disciples after many argumentative flareups with the Pharisees and teachers of the law. At a Jewish festival where water was used, he stood and said in a loud voice: "Let anyone who is thirsty come to me and drink" (John 7:37). Jesus' teaching was dynamic and interactive. It spoke into both the practicalities of everyday life, and into cosmic, eternal issues.

No wonder people were amazed.

We'll best appreciate the Gospels if we understand the forms of Jesus' teaching and the main themes of his teaching. One form was exaggeration or hyperbole. Few believers have ripped out their eyes or cut off their hands because Jesus said in Matthew 5:29-30 that it would be better to do that then end up in eternal condemnation. We understand Jesus' point, made through a shocking statement.

When Jesus said it is easier for a camel to go through the eye of a needle than it is for a rich person to enter God's kingdom, his point was that it is extremely difficult for a self-sufficient person to admit their insufficiency. There is an often-repeated interpretation that in Jerusalem there was a small gate in the wall that necessitated a camel to go to its knees to enter. The problem is, there is no archaeological or epigraphical evidence that any such gate ever existed. Unfortunately, there are many interpretations of Scripture that have been repeated countless times but were never based in fact.

Jesus used similes and metaphors. "I am the light of the world" (John 8:12; 9:5). "I am the true vine" (John 15:1). "You are the light of the world" (Matt. 5:14). These have immediate impact, and they are memorable. Some of his most powerful metaphors explained the kingdom of God. The kingdom is like a mustard seed, leaven, a net, a man who finds a treasure, the sprouting of seed from the soil. These require careful reading. For instance, Jesus did not say the kingdom is like treasure, but it's like what happens when a man finds a treasure and does everything to get it.

Jesus also spoke in short, memorable aphorisms or proverbs. "Do to others as you would have them do to you" (Luke 6:31). "Do not judge, and you will not be judged" (Luke 6:37). "Whoever does the will of my Father in heaven is my brother and sister and mother" (Matt. 12:50). Jesus acknowledged that he spoke figuratively for effect: "Though I have been speaking figuratively, a time is coming when I will no longer use this kind of language but will tell you plainly about my Father" (John 16:25).

Jesus spoke in riddles and he used irony. He used almost every kind of verbal method you could imagine, including parables (which we'll come to in the next chapter). But the power of Jesus' teaching for his original hearers and for us is not in the method. There was a ring of truth, a veracity, and a power in his teaching. For example, Matthew tells us, "When Jesus had finished saying these things, the crowds were amazed at his teaching, because he taught as one who had authority, and not as their teachers of the law" (Matt. 7:28-29). We would have been amazed too.

As with every other kind of text in Scripture, we need to take time to study the context of any given teaching of Jesus. To whom was he speaking? What were the circumstances? Were there any special cultural details? Even in the teaching of Jesus, Scripture means something specific to us that is based in what it meant to Jesus' original audience. That is where we'll find the true meaning, and thus, the authority.

Chapter 18

WHAT WAS JESUS TEACHING IN
THE PARABLES?

For most of us, the parables of Jesus naturally lodge themselves in our memories. The parable of the good Samaritan, for instance, is not only a memorable parable, but it has become embedded in our culture—as in "Good Samaritan laws" that protect people who come to the assistance of others. The parable of the prodigal son—where a foolish young man squanders his inheritance, only to find that his loving father welcomes him back with mercy and grace—is the gospel in a single picture and a simple message: You can come home to God. The lost sheep. The hidden treasure. The wise and foolish virgins. The talents. They are all like pictures on the walls in our homes, memorable scenes that are windows into reality.

Jesus sometimes taught in parables because these vivid stories engage us in thought, emotion, and sensation. They impact us. They force us to go away and ponder, struggling with the meaning perhaps, feeling struck by the truthful and accurate perspective on life they offer. You could say the parables are subversive because they embed themselves in our minds. We cannot escape their message. Jesus said parables unlock mysteries for those who believe, but they remain enigmatic riddles to those who do not have "ears to hear" (Luke 8:8-10). This is one more indication for us that reading Scripture with faith is entirely different from reading it like we read any other book.

We will avoid much frustration and confusion if we remember this: Most parables have one main point. Most of the time the details in the story do not have specific symbolic meaning. In the parable of the good Samaritan (Luke 10), for instance, Jesus did not assign a symbolic meaning to the robbers, the man's wounds, the donkey, the innkeeper, the two silver coins, Jerusalem, or Jericho. Yet that has not prevented Christian thinkers over the centuries from assigning meanings to the details. The problem is, if the meanings are not indicated in the text, such allegorical interpretations are purely arbitrary.

Over the years different people have assigned entirely different meanings to the two coins given to the innkeeper, for instance: they are God the Father and the Son, or they are the Old and New Testaments, or they are the promise of this life and the life to come, etc. But why?

Here again, the simplest and most natural explanation of a biblical text is always the best. The parable of the good Samaritan is Jesus' answer to the question: "Who is my neighbor?" At the end Jesus makes it obvious what his point was:

> "Which of these three do you think was a neighbor to the man who fell into the hands of robbers?"
> The expert in the law replied, "The one who had mercy on him."
> Jesus told him, "Go and do likewise." (Luke 10:36-37)

Parables are not abstract teachings. They almost always call people to a certain response.

Now, if Jesus *did* assign specific meanings to the details in a parable, then of course we must include these in our understanding. In the parable of the sower, for instance, the four landing places of the seed—the path, the rocky ground, the thorns, and the good soil—have specific meanings which Jesus himself indicated (Matt. 13:18-23). The same thing is true of the parable of the weeds (Matt. 13:24-30; 36-43). Nevertheless, even in parables with detailed meaning, we should not lose sight of the forest for the trees. The parable will impact us best if we look for the main point.

As we read the parables, it is also important that we take the time to understand the cultural and geographical settings of the stories. A good commentary, for instance, will describe the road from Jericho to Jerusalem, which is the setting for the good Samaritan story. The "road" is a dusty path winding upwards into the Judean hills through an arid wilderness. It is a lonely and desolate place, where thieves would take advantage of someone. All the parables with agricultural settings are best understood if we understand the life of the farmer in the first century. And shepherding in Jesus' day (as in David's day) is utterly different from ranching today.

The ending is very important. The takeaway from any given parable typically comes in the punch line at the end. The extended parable of the wheat and the weeds, for instance, ends with the day of judgment where truth and falsehood are finally distinguished. In the meantime, we live in the mixture.

The parables of Jesus are God's gift to us who are mere mortals, unable to find truth on our own, and quite lost in interpreting the meaning of life.

"I will open my mouth in parables,
I will utter things hidden since the creation of the
world." (Matt. 13:35)

Chapter 19

WHAT PLACE DOES THE ACTS OF THE APOSTLES PLAY IN THE NEW TESTAMENT?

How shall we describe the amazing narrative we know as The Acts of the Apostles? Fast-paced, expansive, sweeping, intense, surprising, gripping, poignant, compelling, epic? All such descriptions would apply, and more. We have not read Acts rightly if we've just noted a string of historical details. Acts is unique in Scripture, yet it is a continuation of what its Gentile author, Luke, started in his Gospel when he set out to write "an orderly account" for someone named Theophilus so that he "may know the certainty of the things [he had] been taught" (Luke 1:3-4). Acts opens with:

In my former book, Theophilus, I wrote about all that Jesus began to do and to teach until the day he was taken up to heaven, after giving instructions through the Holy Spirit to the apostles he had chosen. (Acts 1:1-2)

Right away Luke tells us the main characters of this narrative are the apostles (including Paul) and the Holy Spirit. From beginning to end, Acts is the story of the Holy Spirit inspiring, empowering, and guiding the followers of Jesus on a world-changing mission.

To read Acts rightly, we need to keep in mind Luke's purpose: to tell the story of how the gospel of Jesus the Christ broke out of the limitations of Judea and Galilee and spread across the Mediterranean world, crossing the barrier between Jew and Gentile and becoming a truly universal spiritual movement. Acts is about gospel and mission and Spirit. It is not a biography about the lives of Peter or John or even the apostle Paul. The focus is on the spread of the message about Jesus, and the dramatic ways people either accepted it or rejected it.

Acts has frequently been read in the past as a description of how the Christian church is supposed to operate. This is understandable, as Christian leaders desire to base today's forms of ministry on a scriptural foundation. Only some of this is possible, however, because Luke clearly did not set out to write a manual on church life or church policy. Yes, it is true that Acts 2 gives a picture of healthy spiritual devotion: "They devoted themselves to the apostles' teaching and to fellowship, to the breaking of bread and to prayer" (v. 42). But a couple of verses later, it says that the believers were selling their property and possessions in order to give to others, that they met in the temple courts every day, and that they ate together in each other's homes (vv. 45-46). Churches today do not follow this pattern detail by detail. We don't sell our cars, there is no temple to meet in every single day, and we don't ring the doorbells of each other's houses every night to share supper. Nor does Acts say these practices were then followed in the churches founded in Asia Minor or Greece or Rome.

Acts tells us what happened, which is not the same thing as telling us what should happen today. There were no church buildings in Acts; no pianos, guitars, or drums for worship. We have descriptions of the baptisms of only first-generation believers, and the method of baptism varied: in the name of Jesus; in the name of Father, Son and Spirit; in bodies of water; in a jail in Philippi; and in the desert along the Gaza road. The leadership structure of the early churches evolved over time, and we are not given a definition of how often the Lord's Supper should take place in our churches today.

Acts is not a list of policies and formulae—it is something more wonderful—an account of the dynamic and oftentimes unpredictable movement of the Spirit of God in the era of the apostles, which puts us in the posture of expecting the unexpected today.

Perhaps there is a lesson in this for us. The vitality of the church will always come from the presence and activity of the Holy Spirit as believers become part of a dynamic movement. This is not to downplay the importance of church structure, but perhaps keep it in perspective.

There are a dizzying number of incidents reported in Acts, each of which is worthy of our contemplation. We ought to put ourselves in Paul's place as he is chased out of a town, or shipwrecked, or plodding through two years of teaching in Ephesus. We need to imagine what it would have been like for Peter, commanded in a dream to enter the home of Cornelius, a Gentile, and witness the unthinkable: the gospel spreading beyond the Jews. We need the maps at the back of our Bibles to have a sense of the geography of this movement.

The structure of Acts can be summed up this way: ever outward. First, there is Jerusalem and the pouring out of the Holy Spirit at Pentecost and the empowering of the apostles. The gospel crosses the line into the Gentile world with Cornelius. Peter is front and center in these early chapters. Then comes the conversion of the hostile Pharisee Saul of Tarsus who became Paul the apostle. The story proceeds with three great missionary journeys crossing one barrier after another until it eventually comes to the seat of the Roman Empire.

The Gospels give the gospel, and Acts, the mission of the gospel. And today in the 21st century, we see the cycle of proclamation, persecution, and expansion repeating. It is important for believers to understand that we have been here before and what it all means.

Chapter 20

HOW SHOULD WE READ
THE EPISTLES OF THE
NEW TESTAMENT?

I was just eight years old at the time, but I still remember the day an irritated elderly lady came storming out of her house to yell at me. I was walking home from our three-room rural elementary school, goofing off with a couple of friends, when I opened the streetside mailbox at a random house and pretended to rifle through my mail—except it wasn't my mail. It was the elderly lady's mail. And she did not think my antics were one bit amusing.

Has it ever occurred to you while reading one of the epistles (letters) in the New Testament that you're reading someone else's mail? In a way we are, and in a way we aren't. For two millennia Christians have read the 20 New Testament epistles as Holy Scripture, as the word of God for us. At the same time, the epistles were personal writings produced for specific people or groups of people, often responding to their particular needs. So we cannot understand the epistles unless we take the effort to discover what lies behind the words.

Some letters read like highly crafted treatises, like the magisterial epistle to the Romans. Others, like 1 and 2 Corinthians, are intricately connected with the needs of a particular group, the believers in the church in Corinth. They had evidently written the apostle Paul and asked specific questions, because he says in 1 Corinthians 7:1, "Now for the matters you wrote about… " and then goes on at some length, responding point by point. Earlier in that same letter, Paul was responding to certain oral reports he'd gotten about what was going on in that complicated and troubled church.

A wide range of circumstances prompted the writing of the epistles. Disorder in a church, the threat of false teaching, trepidation about the end of the world, confusion about death, controversy over religious practices, ambiguity about ethics, weakness in leadership. Some epistles were meant as a word of encouragement or just a way of reconnecting. The books of Hebrews and Romans offer an expansive theological perspective. Some letters focus on a particular theological point: grace in the case of Galatians, Christ in the case of Colossians, the church in the case of Ephesians.

Taken as a whole, these 20 letters add to the Canon of Holy Scripture a multifaceted, real-life description of both faith and behavior.

If you're going to linger in a particular epistle, you will benefit from reading the article about that particular New Testament book in a good Bible dictionary or in the introduction of a commentary. You will get the essential features: who wrote it, to whom it was written, the occasion of its writing, the date, etc. If you are reading an epistle more quickly, the notes in a good study Bible will give you the important facts in brief.

It's best to mediate on some parts of the epistles. For instance, the amazing songs and creeds and prayers embedded in some of them. Other parts of the epistles have complicated details that require the help of Bible linguists, historians, archaeologists, and the like, which we will find in Bible commentaries. If we get the help to understand what "food sacrificed to idols" means in 1 Corinthians 8, we'll be able to learn the lesson there about Christian conscience and freedom. And we cannot understand the epistle of Philemon unless we learn something about slavery in the first century.

Epistles are one genre of Scripture that are best read in long form. Ignore the chapter and verse numbers, which were added to the biblical text in the thirteenth and sixteenth centuries. Reading an epistle straight through is an entirely different experience from reading a few verses at a time. Think of it this way: If you went to your mailbox today and received a multiple-page letter from a beloved relative, you'd read it straight through. You wouldn't read one paragraph today, another tomorrow, and so on. When someone asks you, "Did you get my email yesterday?" try saying, "Yes, and I'm savoring it by reading one sentence a day," and see what response you get. No, we read letters well when we read them naturally.

Reading Scripture in context is a sign of respect for God as much as reading a letter from your mother straight through is a sign of love. The reason, of course, is comprehension. Details at the conclusion of the epistle of Hebrews make the most sense if the start of the epistle is still rattling around in your mind.

The epistles of the New Testament may not have been addressed to us, but they are for us. And we will cherish them as much as—and more than—any letter of love or encouragement a friend ever sent to us.

Chapter 21

WHO WAS PAUL, AND HOW SHOULD WE UNDERSTAND HIS EPISTLES?

Besides Jesus, no single figure was more influential in the beginnings of Christianity than the apostle Paul. Of the 27 books of the New Testament, 13 are attributed to Paul. Take a look at a Bible map showing the missionary journeys of Paul, and you will be astonished to see the territory he covered—not just geographically, but culturally as well.

He was a Jew from the tribe of Benjamin, and he became an impassioned member of the Pharisees (Rom. 11:1; Phil. 3:4-5; Acts 23:6). He came from the city of Tarsus, grew up in the midst of Greco-Roman culture, and was a Roman citizen. This remarkable background meant he was able to speak the gospel into urban settings. He was comfortable in Jerusalem, but also capable of moving into places like Crete, Greece, and Rome. His adaptability was amazing. He spoke with magistrates and philosophers and tradespeople.

His strong views about faith in Christ were most certainly tempered by his dramatic conversion. In the New Testament there is no more radical story of personal change than the story of the young man who was drafted by his fellow Pharisees to actively investigate and prosecute the early followers of Jesus. He stood by as the first Christian martyr, Stephen, was stoned to death. But while traveling to Damascus in Syria to find and arrest more of Jesus' followers, he had a supernatural encounter with Jesus and would soon undergo the utter change of mind and heart, which in his epistles he describes as conversion or repentance.

It wasn't easy for the other apostles to accept this persecutor in their midst, much less endorse him as a teacher. But with the passing of years, Paul eventually set out on his first great journey with a few close companions in tow.

There is quite some variation in the epistles of Paul. Four are called his "prison epistles" because he wrote them from prison (Ephesians, Philippians, Colossians, Philemon). The stress of being in prison comes through at points. For instance, while writing the epistle to his dear friends at Philippi, he believes he may be close to execution.

Of these four, one is written to one person about a runaway slave (Philemon), whereas another, Ephesians, seems to have been written for a whole region of churches.

Three of the epistles, written very late, are usually called "the pastoral epistles" because they contain instructions to Paul's companions Timothy and Titus on how to protect order, harmony, and correct teaching in their churches. Not surprisingly, these are epistles that church leaders look to in shaping ministry roles in congregations. The qualifications for elders and deacons (1 Tim. 3; Titus 1), for instance, describe essential leadership character and are easily applied in our own churches today.

Romans is a powerful, comprehensive description of the whole of the gospel. It covers creation, sin, redemption, and eventual restoration. The special issue of righteousness and grace is emphasized in Romans, as it also is in the epistle of Galatians. First and 2 Corinthians offer great insight into an apostle trying his best to respond to tensions in a troubled church, to challenge bad values, and to call people to action. There is a special poignancy in 2 Corinthians as Paul describes his own hurt through the efforts of those trying to discredit him, and his anxiety about his relationship with the Corinthian church. Here we see the humility of Paul, even as he describes himself as unimpressive in physical appearance and unremarkable as a public speaker. Now that is astonishing to read! The apostle Paul, a so-so preacher.

What should we bear in mind as we read and try to comprehend the epistles of Paul?

In order to understand the epistles of the New Testament, we must begin with context. Every epistle was written to a specific audience and for a specific purpose. If we dig around, we can figure out what false teaching the book of Colossians is countering, what slavery looked like, what family life was like, what the features of the culture were at the time. Then we can ask: "What universal and timeless truths is the author drawing on, truths that apply to us today?"

We may not "greet one another with a holy kiss" (Rom. 16:16) today, but Christian grace and civility still apply. First Peter 3:3 recommends not wearing gold jewelry because in that culture it was ostentatious to do so. Today, avoiding ostentatiousness still applies, though having a gold ring or a gold cross does not rise to that same level. Having elders oversee the ministry of churches today still applies, although having one man appoint them (as Paul instructed Timothy to do) isn't typically the method of selection that is used.

The epistles extend the richness of Holy Scripture, and they remind us once again that the word of God is truth in relationship.

Chapter 22

WHAT IS UNIQUE ABOUT THE BOOKS OF JAMES AND HEBREWS?

We continue to find astonishing variety in the Scriptures when we look at two New Testament books: James, a book of Christian wisdom, and Hebrews, which explains the complicated connections between the old covenant and the new. Both of these books are not addressed to a particular Christian group. They are sometimes called "general epistles."

The epistle of James, which was probably written by the James who was the leader of the church in Jerusalem (Acts 15), focuses on the practicalities of personal and community life. There is nothing in James about the nature of God, the plan of redemption, or the atonement; and Jesus is mentioned only twice. James is almost like the book of Proverbs for the New Testament. Wisdom is not an elite and specialized knowledge, it is everyday practical lifestyle rooted in values that come "from heaven."

> Who is wise and understanding among you? Let them show it by their good life, by deeds done in the humility that comes from wisdom. But if you harbor bitter envy and selfish ambition in your hearts, do not boast about it or deny the truth. Such "wisdom" does not come down from heaven but is earthly, unspiritual, demonic. For where you have envy and selfish ambition, there you find disorder and every evil practice. But the wisdom that comes from heaven is first of all pure; then peace-loving, considerate, submissive, full of mercy and good fruit, impartial and sincere. (James 3:13-17)

This is straightforward and challenging. It is a call to action. If today's leaders would take James' description of wisdom as their paradigm of leadership, our communities would look entirely different. James is also known for the challenge to put faith into action (James 2:14-24). "What good is it... if someone claims to have faith but has no deeds?" (2:14). James confronts favoritism, greed, and destructive talk. James gives some perspective for those going through trials or who are teetering on the edge of temptation. James challenges us to be patient, respectful, and peace-loving.

The greatest challenge in reading the epistle of James is not so much understanding what it means, but living what it prescribes.

The book of Hebrews is long for an epistle. It is steeped in details about the Old Testament sacrificial system and explanations of how the plan of redemption has been fulfilled in Jesus. It is a mystery who authored this book. "To the Hebrews," means it was written for Jewish Christians who especially needed a theological explanation of how faith in Christ fulfilled the Old Testament law.

The first 10 chapters describe how Christ and faith in Christ has superseded the old covenant, has surpassed the accomplishments of Moses and Joshua, and has replaced the priesthood and the sacrificial system.

Therefore, since we have a great high priest who has ascended into heaven, Jesus the Son of God, let us hold firmly to the faith we profess. For we do not have a high priest who is unable to empathize with our weaknesses, but we have one who has been tempted in every way, just as we are—yet he did not sin. Let us then approach God's throne of grace with confidence, so that we may receive mercy and find grace to help us in our time of need. (Heb. 4:14-16)

The book of Hebrews provides a key to unlocking challenging questions about the story of God in which he works for centuries in and through a special covenant people, starting with Abraham, but then does something entirely new in Jesus. It is not that the terms of a relationship with God have changed, which always was and always will be faith based on grace. But the scope of God's grace now expands to the whole world with the atonement in Jesus.

The book of Hebrews also warns believers about falling away from the faith, and challenges them to persevere in difficult circumstances, remaining faithful to the new covenant. Hebrews 11 is a stunning description of how faith and hope across the ages have been the distinguishing characteristics of God's people, beginning with Abraham. "Now faith is confidence in what we hope for and assurance about what we do not see. This is what the ancients were commended for" (Heb. 11:1-2). The followers of Jesus have, in his sacrifice, the power to overcome sin and to persevere:

> Therefore, since we are surrounded by such a great cloud of witnesses, let us throw off everything that hinders and the sin that so easily entangles. And let us run with perseverance the race marked out for us, fixing our eyes on Jesus, the pioneer and perfecter of faith. For the joy set before him he endured

the cross, scorning its shame, and sat down at the right hand of the throne of God. (Heb. 12:1-2)

To understand Hebrews, we have to look backwards into the Old Testament, seeing how spiritual realities are anticipated and then fulfilled. When we do that, we will be stunned by the wide scope of biblical truth in the great narrative that stretches from a covenant with Bedouin shepherds from Mesopotamia to the entire world. And Hebrews lets us know that taking the long view—of persevering and plodding, of believing and behaving rightly—always has been the way of God with men and women.

Chapter 23

HOW SHOULD WE UNDERSTAND
THE BOOK OF REVELATION?

If we did not realize already that it takes a lifetime to understand the Bible (and that's a good thing), the point is driven home when we get to the last book in the Bible—Revelation. It starts out simply enough, it is a "revelation (in Greek, *apocalypse*) from Jesus Christ," it is a "prophecy," and it comes as a letter to seven churches. Fair enough, but then come the angels, beasts, earthquakes, horses and riders, wars, thrones, and much more. What are we to make of all this?

Here are two unhelpful approaches to Revelation. One is to think it is such an incomprehensible book of enigmas and riddles that we avoid it. The second is to uncritically follow someone else's arbitrary interpretation of all the details and hidden meanings of its passages. Revelation is not too hard to comprehend, and we should benefit from it. But first we need to understand the big picture.

Revelation never describes itself as a symbolic code of future events plotted on a timeline, though it does guide us regarding the future. Like the books of prophecy in the Old Testament, Revelation proclaims a message. In Revelation the message is that God is coming to judge and to redeem, and that the powers of evil and empires will clash before God establishes the fullness of his kingdom. That central message gives people two things: *warnings* and *comfort*, just as the Old Testament books of prophecy did.

If we keep our eyes on this central message and the intended effects, we will be less likely to get bogged down when we get into details in the book.

The book of Revelation is similar to other literature of the time that's called "apocalyptic," which typically includes visions, global clashes, end-of-the-world warnings, and many, many symbols. It is, of course, the cryptic symbolism of Revelation that makes it challenging to understand. But when we connect many of the symbols with elements that appear earlier in the Old Testament Prophets Isaiah, Jeremiah, Ezekiel, and Daniel, the message emerges from the details.

A commentary that many have found very helpful is *The Message of Revelation: I Saw Heaven Opened*, by Michael Wilcock (part of *The Bible Speaks Today* series).

Like the other commentaries in this series, the focus is on the message of the book. Here is how Wilcock outlines the flow of Revelation:

1:1-8	The Prologue
1:9–3:22	Scene 1: The Church in the World
4:1–8:1	Scene 2: Suffering for the Church
8:2–11:18	Scene 3: Warning for the World
11:19–15:4	Scene 4: The Drama of History
15:5–16:21	Scene 5: Punishment for the World
17:1–19:10	Scene 6: Babylon the Whore
19:11–21:8	Scene 7: The Drama Behind History
21:9–22:19	Scene 8: Jerusalem the Bride
22:20–21	The Epilogue

The number seven appears many times in the book, 54 times altogether, and it is obvious that most of the book is organized around cycles of seven. Seven proclamations to seven churches (chapters 2–3), and three sets of seven-part visionary narratives: the seven seals (4:1–8:1), the seven trumpets (8:2–11:18), and the seven bowls (15:5–16:21).

Nothing in the book of Revelation suggests that its sequence of symbols and visions are to be plotted along a chronological timeline, all related strictly to the very end of human history. Christians in the first few generations saw the descriptions of persecution against God's people as exactly what they were experiencing, for instance, at the end of the first century during the reign of Roman Emperor Domitian. Christians today who experience the spiritual battles of persecution, sometimes at the hands of national, totalitarian powers, read Revelation as a letter to them.

The three sets of seven (seals, trumpets, bowls) may best be read as three great cycles of bloody conflict and victory, each rising to a higher level of intensity. Here Revelation is not just describing what will happen in the future, but what does happen in history and will continue happening until the end.

The end of the story is an astonishing description of a new creation, including symbols of a new city, a new temple, and a new people. The message is this: God will prevail. A day is coming when "There will be no more death or mourning or crying or pain, for the old order of things has passed away" (21:4). The ultimate victory of God is a closeness and a communion with his people.

What can we do to understand the book of Revelation? Reading it straight through in one, two, or three settings is very helpful because you will see connections. Read it in different translations. And sometime read it alongside one of the better commentaries.

Part IV

INTERPRETING THE BIBLE

Chapter 24

WHAT IS THE MOST NATURAL
WAY TO READ THE BIBLE?

I shudder to think how close I came to giving up on the Bible. Like many people, I tried for years to read Scripture in ways that were doomed to fail. My way of reading made the Bible hard to understand, and it made me think this book was perhaps too inscrutable or too out of date for me to pay attention to it. Yes, it was convenient when other people picked out the good bits and made juicy quotes just perfect for a bumper sticker: "The LORD is my shepherd" (Ps. 23:1), "Do not worry about tomorrow" (Matt. 6:34), "Take delight in the LORD, and he will give you the desires of your heart" (Ps. 37:4).

And then there is, "God helps those who help themselves." Oops! That's not actually in the Bible. But like many biblically illiterate people, I thought it was.

This was dangerous. I was missing the word of God. Worst, I was misinterpreting the word of God because when we quote a verse out of context, we usually twist its true meaning and use it to reinforce our preconceptions. The solution is to read Scripture on its own terms. To read it widely and repeatedly. To accept the fact that these are ancient documents written in a time and place far removed, and so it takes patience and work to understand. But as any gold miner knows, it is worth as much time and effort as it takes to get gold out of the mine.

What is the most natural way to read the Bible?

1. *We need to learn the context of the particular biblical book we are reading*. We read Jeremiah differently than we read Ephesians or Revelation. These are all the word of God, but given to us through the words of three very different men in different circumstances. If you have a good study Bible, all you need to do is carefully read the introduction at the start of the book, where the biblical scholars will outline the author, circumstances, and content. Look up the biblical book in a Bible dictionary or encyclopedia, and you will get much more information—and more yet if you read the introduction in a commentary.

2. *Read the translation that you can understand and that motivates you to keep reading.* Remember, the best translation for you is the one you'll actually read. There have been times in my life when reading a thought-by-thought translation was the best thing to do (see chapter 4 on translations), and other times reading a word-for-word translation. It is best to settle into one version you'll typically read and reread.

3. *Read at a reasonable pace and try to ignore the chapter and verse numbers.* We would all understand the Bible much better if we read it freely and naturally, rather than like a step-by-step instruction manual. When you get a letter from a friend or relative, you just sit down and read it through because that is the best way to understand his or her message. No one watches movies in five-minute installments, and no one would say that after viewing still photos of a movie, you have seen that movie. Yet reading a "verse of the day" is very popular. If you take 20 minutes instead of 5 to read a biblical book, you will get through Romans in three sittings, Genesis in about six sittings, and many biblical books, like the epistles, in single sittings. Reading for comprehension is all about synthesis—connecting all the small ideas with the large controlling ideas. The payoff is enormous.

4. *Follow a reading plan.* No one wants to open the Bible randomly each day and read what is there. There are many excellent reading plans that organize a comprehensive reading of Scripture. Some go from Genesis to Revelation, but many help the reader by moving about the Bible, going back and forth in the Old and New Testaments, for instance. Many offer a way to read the whole Bible in a year. This is not too difficult. It takes only 15 minutes a day.

However, this is the key: Don't get bogged down when you're doing that 15 minutes of reading and you are having a hard time understanding it. This is why most people give up. Just keep reading. Read if you understand and read if you're in a passage you do not understand. If you are reading the word of God as a lifestyle, you'll come back to that passage again and again. It may be that you'll understand it the fourth time you read it, or you'll understand it when you get to the end of the book. If you have doubts you'll be able to be committed to reading 15 minutes a day, then choose a two-year reading plan, which takes just seven minutes a day.

Look at it this way: God is there for you for your whole life. On good days and bad days. And the word of God is there for you for your whole life. Just read. Just read. Just read.

Chapter 25

HOW CAN WE HEAR GOD'S VOICE IN SCRIPTURE?

Some years back, I did a survey of our church's congregation with the simple question: "If you could ask God one thing, what would it be?" I was not surprised that the most frequent response had to do with the problem of evil in the world, but I was struck by the next most common question: "How can I hear the voice of God?" The various wording people used indicated some were facing important decisions, others wanted to know if their lives were "on track" with God, some were in crisis, and still others expressed feelings of spiritual isolation and just wanted to "hear" from God.

There is a long history and many debates about how God "speaks" to us. Our concern in this chapter is how God speaks in and through Holy Scripture. This must be the believer's major conviction, that we find the voice of God in Scripture, and that the authority of the Bible trumps all other claims about hearing God. Throughout Scripture, God is talking. Creation took place at the verbal command of God. The Hebrews became a nation when they met their God at Mount Sinai and he spoke to them through Moses. The prophets' oracles often began with: "This is what the LORD says."

And the Gospels proclaim a whole new form of the voice of God: "In the beginning was the Word, and the Word was with God, and the Word was God" (John 1:1). Or, as the opening words of the book of Hebrews puts it: "In the past God spoke to our ancestors through the prophets at many times and in various ways, but in these last days he has spoken to us by his Son" (Heb. 1:1-2).

Whenever we find ourselves longing to hear the voice of God—wanting to know if we're doing the right thing, or yearning to know that we are not alone—we must remember this: We have in Scripture thousands and thousands of expressions of the will and the ways of God. We have an analysis of life that is complex and refined, giving us concrete moral instruction and wisdom-based ethics. We have "the mind of Christ" (1 Cor. 2:16). We have the "wisdom from above" (James 3:17 ESV). We have "Spirit-taught words" (1 Cor. 2:13). Do you want to hear God's voice?

Then take in what he says in his Word. Drink deeply. Study well. Meditate slowly. Keep starting over.

It may be that the most relevant question for us is not "Where can we find the voice of God?" but "What prevents us from taking in the voice of God?" Many biblical passages speak to that.

Listening to the voice of God is risky. At Mount Sinai the people said to Moses, "Speak to us yourself and we will listen. But do not have God speak to us or we will die" (Ex. 20:19). Moses replied that the fear of God would be good for them; it would keep them from sinning, although it will sting at times.

There are many passages that say we resist listening to God because we know obedience is the next step. In the parable of the soils, Jesus analyzes why the word of God (the seed) does not take root. Shallow acceptance (the rocky ground), and the competition of worries and money (the thorny soil) get in the way. But simple lack of understanding (the path) thwarts a person's spiritual life.

How can we hear God's voice in Scripture? It isn't really complicated. We need to read it. We need to do the work to understand it (which is the point of this whole book). And we need to have the right heart attitude, which is more challenging than anything else. We have to honestly admit that we will resist being obedient to God, and that we will be tempted to make the Bible mean what we want it to mean. That prospect should terrify us. Putting our words into the mouth of God is the height of arrogance.

Here is a caution. For years I sat in Bible studies where the leader read a passage and then asked the group: "What does this mean to you?" Only much later did I learn (and it made perfect sense when I did) that the meaning of Scripture does not flow from the subjective experience of the believer. The question is not "What does this mean to me?" but rather "What does this mean?"

When the apostle Paul said, "I myself in my mind am a slave to God's law, but in my sinful nature a slave to the law of sin" (Rom. 7:25), he meant something specific. It is our obligation to dig and dig until we learn what he meant, and then talk about how it applies to us.

There is only one way to receive the pure and powerful truth of God—and that is to seek to understand what the Bible meant so we can apply what it means to our lives today.

Chapter 26

WHAT ARE THE PROPER WAYS
TO APPLY SCRIPTURE
TO LIFE TODAY?

It is dangerous to understand the Bible better. It is all too easy for us to feel just a bit of pride about pulling out the meaning of biblical texts, as if we were beginning to master the Scriptures when, of course, exactly the opposite is the whole point. The temptation may come from the power we may feel from having "spiritual knowledge," which can move us from insecurity to superiority. Or we may want to put ourselves over Scripture so we don't need to obey it. As Paul says, "knowledge puffs up" (1 Cor. 8:1).

Here are a few of the reasons why many biblical authors charge us with not just *knowing* the word of God, but *practicing* it.

God (through Moses):

Fix these words of mine in your hearts and minds; tie them as symbols on your hands and bind them on your foreheads. Teach them to your children, talking about them when you sit at home and when you walk along the road, when you lie down and when you get up. Write them on the doorframes of your houses and on your gates. (Deut. 11:18-20)

Jesus:

"Therefore everyone who hears these words of mine and puts them into practice is like a wise man who built his house on the rock. The rain came down, the streams rose, and the winds blew and beat against that house; yet it did not fall, because it had its foundation on the rock. But everyone who hears these words of mine and does not put them into practice is like a foolish man who built his house on sand. The rain came down, the streams rose, and the winds blew and beat against that house, and it fell with a great crash." (Matt. 7:24-27)

Paul:

All Scripture is God-breathed and is useful for teaching, rebuking, correcting and training in righteousness, so that the servant of God may be thoroughly equipped for every good work. (2 Tim. 3:16-17)

And using a mirror for a wonderful analogy, James charges us:

Do not merely listen to the word, and so deceive yourselves. Do what it says. Anyone who listens to the word but does not do what it says is like someone who looks at his face in a mirror and, after looking at himself, goes away and immediately forgets what he looks like. But whoever looks intently into the perfect law that gives freedom, and continues in it—not forgetting what they have heard, but doing it—they will be blessed in what they do. (James 1:22-25)

These and many other passages suggest that applying Scripture begins with assimilating its content. Reading, meditating, discussing, practicing, praying, and memorizing are all ways for the biblical text to form the spiritual muscle tissue of our lives. This is not about having a list of verses rattling around in our heads, but having the shape and motion of our lives formed by biblical truth.

Much of this book has been about personal reading and comprehension of Scripture, but this is a good place to mention the power of group or community Bible discussion. It is enormously formative to discuss the meaning and application of Scripture in some kind of group. We see new things through the eyes of other people, especially those brave enough to share how their life's difficulties connect or clash with biblical truths.

It is possible for a Bible group to wallow in ignorance if the mode of operation is to read a biblical text and throw it open to the group with the question: "What does this mean to you?" No! A biblical text means something specific, intended by the original author. Someone in a group Bible study needs to take responsibility to study these things ahead of time and dig out the meaning.

In the group setting, the question can and should be: "How do you see this applying to your life?" A biblical text means something specific, but it may be applied in many different directions, as long as the application is really connected with the meaning.

That raises another question: Can a biblical text motivate someone, even if the meaning and application don't seem to be connected? The story can be told many times over, for instance, of someone reading one of the great missionary texts in Acts and believing God told him, through the text, to pack his bags and go overseas. It certainly is possible that the Holy Spirit guides someone through the words or sentiment of a biblical text—even if the text isn't properly applied to everyone in that specific way. Such experiences are not about the meaning of a biblical text, nor its typical application, but a unique guidance of the Spirit for a particular person.

So the norm is this: biblical text first, original meaning next, and finally, present-day application. In this process we learn and relearn "Your word, LORD, is eternal" (Ps. 119:89).

Chapter 27

HOW CAN WE REFINE OUR UNDERSTANDING OF BIBLICAL THEOLOGY?

Theology is not limited to the work of professors and clergy. Any serious Christian who has invested time in reading and studying Scripture is doing the work of theology, because theology (from the Greek words *theos*, meaning "God," and *logia*, meaning "utterance, speech, reasoning") is simply seeking ways to understand and speak about God, and all else in life as God defines it.

This is one of the enormous blessings of being a lifetime reader of Scripture. We are learning God. And learning everything God has said about everything else that really matters in life. *What is a person? Why are people violent? What does a good marriage look like? What is our relationship with the animal kingdom? What happens after we die? How can we find peace and prosperity in life? Why does money become a source of tension? Where can we find justice?*

What Scripture offers us, in its totality, is a comprehensive knowledge about God and life. This knowledge is not unlimited, for mysteries remain. Believers should not be frustrated by that. The Bible should never be criticized for not being what it never claims to be. It is not a comprehensive textbook of science. It does not address all areas of economics and government. The Bible is not a documentary of all the details of the historical periods it addresses, but rather, the telling of the story of God's interaction with humanity.

So how do we, in our quest to reason about and speak about God, refine a "biblical theology"? First, we should not rely on the longstanding method of searching for verses, producing a list, and pretending that this produces a coherent and true doctrine or theology. It is easy, of course, to use a concordance or a computer program or an online lookup function to put in front of our eyeballs all of the biblical verses that use the words *heaven, sin, Christ, baptism, money,* or *violence*. While this can be a helpful exercise, creating such lists does not render overarching, rational concepts. If we are trying to figure out what the Bible says about violence, we will have to find the passages that offer major insights, and those passages may not even use the word *violence* at all—for instance, Cain murdering Abel (Gen. 4:8). It is helpful to do word searches, but only as part of a larger strategy of refining your understanding of biblical theology.

Theology is all about synthesis, which is to take many ideas and discover their connections, leading to an overall theory or system. We sometimes talk about our "belief system," which is what theology leads to, and it is a wonderful thing. Biblically knowledgeable believers are not shocked when people lie, steal, and cheat. When wars break out. When people are used as slaves. We understand these harsh realities because the word of God describes the causes and development of sin—and our understanding is our "theology." This understanding does not come from looking up the word *sin* online. Rather, as we read all of Scripture as a lifestyle, we discover and synthesize thousands of places where "sin" is described as transgression, stumbling, iniquity, wandering, crookedness, trespass, impiety, lawlessness, injustice, and more. The Psalms talk about brokenness. Jesus teaches about blindness. Revelation points to evil. Read Scripture as a lifestyle and you lose your naiveté—and that is a good thing.

Maturity is all about synthesis—putting together what you learned years ago, with what you learned months ago, with what you learned today. You see patterns of life. Lessons that are cumulative. So it is with refining a biblical theology. The most important thing we do is read Scripture regularly, widely (not just the parts we like), and for a lifetime. Synthesis happens in our minds automatically. You read along and your mind is picking up bits and pieces of the truth about love, and righteousness, and temptation, and angels, and God, and a thousand other ideas. In the back of your mind, connections are forming. Every time you come back to a certain biblical book, you see things you never did before, but the connections get stronger. You understand Jeremiah's "new covenant" because you recall the prior covenants with Abraham, Moses, and others, and you remember Jesus and the book of Hebrews' teaching about the "new covenant." And so it is with hundreds of other big ideas.

So the main commitment we need to make for the big payoff of gaining a substantial "belief system" is the faithful and thoughtful reading of all of Scripture. The synthesis will happen in our minds. But to ensure that we are reading with understanding and effect, we need to read with concentration. Taking notes is extremely helpful. Just have pen and paper nearby when you read. Note a verse that strikes you, a question that comes to mind, a connection or contrast with another passage, something you want to remember, a thought you want to tell someone else. Do that as a lifestyle and the synthesis will go deeper. Review your notes months later, and you will make connections that are just waiting to happen.

Truth is too good to be viewed as a list. The word of God offers a faithful description of reality. The difference between a flourishing and a failing life frequently hinges on where we have made the effort to discover and live in reality. This is why we want to understand Scripture.

Chapter 28

HOW CAN WE KNOW IF
SOMEONE IS GIVING
FALSE TEACHING?

When I was young in the faith, I had a deep hunger to find the truth of God because I had tasted it, it was deeply satisfying, and I sensed that my soul was just waiting to be revived from some kind of hibernation. So I sought out different Christian teachers and preachers, read some best-selling books, and sampled Christian radio teaching. But I was unsettled by the feeling I sometimes had that the Bible teaching I was hearing seemed only loosely linked with the biblical text, and it was peculiar, out of sync, and did not have the "ring of truth" I experienced when reading Scripture itself.

Some years later, I came to the conclusion that the "smell test" needs to be taken seriously. If we are exposed to teaching that just doesn't "smell" right, then we ought to proceed carefully. Maybe the teaching is sound and we just need to get in sync with it, or it may be that our "noses" are all right and we're hearing that most dangerous thing—false teaching.

The Bible itself speaks of "false teaching." There is a difference between truth and falsehood, and when it comes to Bible interpretation, there is a lot of teaching that is garbage—and it smells that way.

So how can we know if someone is giving false teaching from the Bible?

First, we need to watch out for *opportunists*. Teachers who gain illicitly from their teaching need to be avoided. It is amazing, really, how many masses of people will follow someone who is manipulative, grossly greedy, and dishonest. They promise prosperity if others make them prosperous, and they laugh all the way to the bank. The short epistle of Jude offers a stark analysis of this kind of false teaching:

These people are blemishes at your love feasts, eating with you without the slightest qualm—shepherds who feed only themselves. They are clouds without rain, blown along by the wind; autumn trees, without fruit and uprooted—twice dead. They are wild waves of the sea, foaming up their shame; wandering stars, for whom blackest darkness has been reserved forever. ... These people are grumblers and faultfinders; they follow their own evil desires; they boast about themselves and flatter others for their own advantage. (Jude 12-13, 16)

This is a stunning description of the destructive effects of "shepherds who feed only themselves." The passage indicates that we must watch out for the selfishness, fruitlessness, chaos, and arrogance of certain people. They gain influence via their sheer conceit. Ironically, we give them credence on the basis of their pride, the character flaw that most disqualifies them. When we realize we have been sucked in by this kind of false teacher, we need to do some soul-searching to figure out why.

Another kind of false teaching is *ill-founded speculation*. Some people make a career out of spouting details of topics like spiritual life or prophesy or cosmology, which go way beyond what Scripture actually teaches. There are no controls on such speculation. Sometimes the motive is manipulation—esoteric knowledge can be a power tactic. The last sentence of 1 Timothy is this plea:

O Timothy, guard the deposit entrusted to you. Avoid the irreverent babble and contradictions of what is falsely called "knowledge," for by professing it some have swerved from the faith.   (1 Tim. 6:20-21 ESV)

Second Timothy contains a similar warning:

Charge them before God not to quarrel about words, which does no good, but only ruins the hearers. Do your best to present yourself to God as one approved, a worker who has no need to be ashamed, rightly handling the word of truth. But avoid irreverent babble, for it will lead people into more and more ungodliness, and their talk will spread like gangrene. (2 Tim. 2:14-17 ESV)

A third kind of false teaching is *legalism*. Jesus confronted this distortion of the truth of God when he exposed the corrupt side of sectarianism: "Woe to you Pharisees, because you give God a tenth of your mint, rue and all other kinds of garden herbs, but you neglect justice and the love of God" (Luke 11:42). First Timothy 4:3 warns about teachers who "forbid people to marry and order them to abstain from certain foods, which God created to be received with thanksgiving by those who believe and who know the truth."

These and other forms of false teaching all have causes, and sometimes we will avoid spiritual collisions if we see them ahead of time. False teaching can come from naiveté, arrogance, or selfish gain. The problem we face today is that it isn't hard to grab a microphone, create a webpage, or even self-publish a book. We must make careful choices about whom we listen to, and have the strength to turn away when a suspicious teacher is tickling our ears and offering false comfort.

Chapter 29

WHAT ARE SOME GOOD PLANS AND DISCIPLINES FOR READING SCRIPTURE?

I still cherish my boyhood memories of going fishing with my grandfather. It seems like it was yesterday. One day while I was sorting through the wide variety of tackle I had collected, fidgeting with lures and sinkers and bobbers and the rest in my fancy tackle box, my grandfather looked at me and said: "Mel, you won't catch a thing unless your hook is in the water." Of course, he was right. His hook was always in the water, and he had much more to show for it.

The main principle of reading Scripture for a lifetime of spiritual growth is: just read it. Don't spend too much time looking for the "just right" study Bible, or other helps. Don't neglect reading Scripture because you are in a period when you are having a hard time understanding it. And don't slow down because you have not found a plan that is right for you. Put your hook in the water. Something will happen.

Here are some guidelines for a lifestyle of fruitful Bible reading.

1. *Follow a plan, but vary the plan year by year.* There are plans that are structured for reading the whole Bible in a year, or two years. The plan may go from Genesis to Revelation, but some plans have you read an Old Testament portion, a New Testament portion, and a Psalm every day, for instance. One very ambitious plan has you reading the whole Bible in 90 days. I like doing that every couple of years. It takes me about a half-hour of reading a day. One plan gets you through the four Gospels in 40 days. Another goes through just the New Testament in a year. There are holiday reading plans for Lent or Advent which really help us focus on the birth, death, and resurrection of Christ. You can find verse-of-the-day devotions, but they are of limited worth because you do not get the broad scope of the story of Scripture. BibleGateway.com is a good place to find a wide variety of plans.

2. *Do not give up.* If you start a reading plan in January and falter in March, getting hopelessly behind the plan, just choose another plan for the year. Keep your hook in the water. If all else fails, just read a chapter a day. Consider a day incomplete unless you read *something* in Scripture.

3. *Use a simple tool for a schedule.* I like printing out a plan on a single sheet of paper and having it tucked in the back of my Bible. You can use an online scheduling function on your computer or mobile device, but make sure it is a function that is easy to use and easy to access.

4. *Decide whether you will make notes or not.* Writing your thoughts and questions down as you read helps with comprehension, and many people do it faithfully. I have generally preferred not doing that, however, because I know I will keep reading every day if it is just me and the Bible in my hand. It is different when I am studying Scripture for a group I am in or a teaching I am preparing in which case I take careful notes. You should figure out what works best for you. If taking notes does not bog you down, do it. You will have an accumulating treasure.

5. *Know the time of day that is best for you, and set a pattern.* This is really important. Lifestyle is about regularity. Most people eat and sleep on a preferred pattern that works for them. So it is with reading Scripture as a lifestyle. I like the early morning when it is quiet in the house and my to-do list isn't pressing in on my mind. Others find a lunch break or the evening better.

6. *Read introductions to Bible books.* If you've gotten through Numbers and are ready to dive into Deuteronomy, don't just plow ahead. Take a few minutes to read an introduction which will orient you to the context, circumstances, date, themes, and author of what you are about to read. Study Bibles, for instance, have concise introductions that are no more than a page. But you can get longer introductions in Bible dictionaries or handbooks.

7. *Allow time for reflection.* In today's hectic world this gets squeezed out, but it is essential. This may mean shutting your Bible, closing your eyes for five minutes and thinking about what you're read, speaking to God a word of thanks or frustration or inquiry. I find taking a walk after reading to be an excellent way to let the thoughts circulate around in my mind. If there is a single verse, or even just a phrase or a single word, that strikes you powerfully, take some time to ponder it. God the Holy Spirit may be placing a marker in your mind which will be important at some later point in your life. Commit to this: read *and* reflect.

Chapter 30

A FINAL WORD ABOUT FAITH

One day some religious people, a group known as the Sadducees, tried to draw Jesus into a theological trap on a speculative question about the afterlife. Instead of answering their question directly, Jesus said: "You are in error because you do not know the Scriptures or the power of God." That was a shocking confrontation. These people knew the Hebrew Scriptures very well. It was their profession and their preoccupation. But because they were using the word of God instead of trusting it, Jesus told them they quite simply didn't "know" it.

This book is called *How to Understand the Bible*, but it could have been called *How to Understand the Bible in a Way that is Accurate According to the Standards of Lan-*

guage and that is Faithful According to God's Intent. (In prior centuries book titles were sometimes that long!)

In order to get out of Scripture all that is there for us, we have to read it both as an ordinary text, and an extraordinary one. This is not a contradiction. We must follow the rules that apply to ordinary language because this word of God came to us in the ordinary forms of letters and oracles, poetry and proverb, simile and metaphor, and all the other ordinary ways ordinary words work. We must read Scripture naturally, in other words, and not by some artificial assumptions about the words of the Bible. It is all-important, for instance, for us to read portions of Scripture in their context because words have meaning only in context. We expect other people to understand what we say in context out of fairness, not quoting us in a way that misrepresents us. We should show God the same respect. We like to quote individual Bible verses as answers to complex problems, but our application of a verse is only as good as our understanding the verse in context. No prophet or apostle would have ever conceived of his oracle or epistle chopped up into such tiny bits.

We must also read Scripture with eyes of faith as a body of extraordinary texts. Not everybody who reads the Bible considers it the Holy Bible or the word of God. But if you do, that will shape your understanding.

The Christian thinker Anselm of Canterbury (c. 1033-1109) famously said: "I believe in order that I may understand" (*Credo ut intelligam*). The principle is otherwise known as "faith seeking understanding," as it was expressed by Augustine of Hippo in the fourth century.

Putting it simply, these leading thinkers and many others have said it is when our lives are connected with our Creator, when our minds and hearts are awakened to his power and presence, when we are "believers," that we will begin to understand the way things really are.

Knowing the Bible is not the ultimate objective. Knowing God is. Really knowing God. And knowing God via the revelation God has given of himself, not our imaginary constructs. This is exciting! When we commit ourselves to knowing the Scriptures, we are truly embarking on a life-transforming experience. And the real beginning is when we say, "I believe..."

For more resources, including downloadable
group discussion guide...

www.WordWay.org

43988357R00089

Made in the USA
Lexington, KY
19 August 2015

This book is dedicated to my wife, Christy. Your undying support keeps me going every day and I'm forever grateful.

It's also dedicated to my sons Jacob, Luke, and Ben. You inspire me daily.

HERE'S WHAT'S INSIDE

PREFACE

I was bitten by the digital marketing bug in 2011. For years I worked at a company that served clients in the public-speaking niche. We taught business owners how to collect leads and make sales from their public speeches.

It worked well for many years… but a change was coming.

It was hard to attract, incentivize, and retain quality employees that could drive consistent results without getting burned out. Also, hungry, commissioned sales reps would take the stack of leads and cherry-pick the hottest ones to call, ignoring the rest. We didn't have a predictable way to market to those that weren't ready to buy at the moment.

Further, a completely offline approach to marketing and sales wasn't keeping up with the times. Not only were buyers falling through the cracks, but it also became harder to reach them on the phone.

It was at this time that I was introduced to digital marketing and everything changed.

A few years later I found myself at the same company but now responsible for executing the digital strategy for us and for our coaching clients (online ads, event registrations, course sales, list growth ... you name it). I built lots of online marketing systems that grossed nearly seven figures in the first year alone.

I was hooked. I had cracked the code of high-converting sales systems, also known as funnels.

I also began to notice a gap in the marketplace. I had a theory that I could leverage the skills I was using for the company and our coaching clients and start my own business doing marketing and ads for others.

I had never been more scared or excited.

After an eleven-year run at my former company, I took the leap of faith and started a marketing agency, Red Anchor Marketing, LLC in January of 2017.

I didn't have a list of people to call on but I *did* have a powerful skill set. I could take any idea, in any niche, and take it to the marketplace quickly for testing. I didn't need to take months of development time, no coding, no copywriters ... I was building funnels.

As with any new business, it wasn't always smooth sailing. I had some false starts and some do-overs along the way, but ultimately I figured it out and the agency took off.

Since 2011 I've built hundreds of funnels that have generated millions of dollars and hundreds of thousands of leads for me and my clients.

I developed a system, which I'm about to teach you, to build funnels quickly and profitably so you can get the ideas out of your head and in front of your ideal customers.

I've taught the system to my friends and team members and got them great results, too.

Here's what some of them had to say:

"This takes the headache out of figuring out what to say and do and where to put everything ... it's a step-by-step process ... Without this, I would spend hours working on my funnel, only to watch it spiral out of control ..."

"I would highly recommend the One Hour Funnel™ System to anyone who was lost like I was in the world of digital marketing. I literally knew nothing about funnels when I began and then halfway through, I had acquired so much knowledge that I started a new side company selling the information in my brain and using Cody's methodology to put it to market."

"This is a total game changer. Now I know what to say and where to say it so it creates interest in what I have to say. Thanks for helping me understand how to do that. I have my ads going, and I'm already starting to get new leads and I know that it's going to lead to an influx of new business."

In May of 2018 I wanted to take all the mystery out of funnel-building and went live on Facebook for thirty-one days in a row and built funnels from scratch. To check that out go to my Facebook page at facebook.com/codyburchdigital/.

Here's the thing—funnels have completely changed my life. They've helped me build a great business and I know they can do the same for you, too.

Cody Burch

My name is Cody Burch and I'm going to teach you how to bring your ideas to life so you can predictably and systematically grow your leads and sales. In this book, I reveal the nine-step process to creating your *own* high-converting and profitable sales funnel in only an hour.

A few years back, I saw a video about "the richest place on the planet." You might think it's New York City, Dubai, or Shanghai, but you'd be wrong. The richest place on the planet is the graveyard.

It's a morbid thought, but I agree. How many ideas were never brought to life? How many songs or poems went unwritten? Words that were never spoken? Big business ideas that could have saved a life, changed someone's future, rescued someone from poverty or a job they hate, but they were never expressed . . .

It seemed too hard.

They didn't know where to start.

The list goes on and on.

I don't want that to happen to you. I'm going to show you the proven system I use every time to get ideas out into the world so they can go to work, solve problems, and help people.

THE ONE HOUR FUNNEL

What's Your Ideal Sales Process?

I f you sell something—a service, product, or even an idea—in the marketplace, what are the ideal steps that a customer would take in exchange for money?

If you mapped it out, what would it look like?

First off, you'd probably ask yourself, "Who is that person?"

What are they like? What do they believe about your solution that may or may not be true? What have they tried in the past that didn't work? What alternatives exist outside of *your* thing?

We'll unpack the idea of your market in the next chapter, but it's useful to pause for a minute and imagine that person.

Second, what would you want them to know about your solution?

Imagine you're sitting at your local coffee shop. It's packed. You're making your third attempt to connect your iPad to the Wi-Fi and gently blowing the foam off your cappuccino.

A stranger walks up, notices the empty seat across from you and, it being standing-room only, asks if they may have a seat. You oblige. They sit.

You exchange pleasantries and notice they are shifting in their chair and wincing every few seconds. You're not sure what's wrong with them but they are clearly uncomfortable.

Your curiosity overtakes you after the fifth pain-filled adjustment. "You alright?"

They wince one more time and painfully shake their head back and forth.

Your new friend goes on to complain about their back pain. They can't sleep, they can't work, they can't sit comfortably in the coffee shop.

Now imagine that you were a back pain specialist. You could help them overcome their pain with 100% certainty and effectiveness. Imagine you had developed a new process with breakthrough technology and a ten-week program that would both give them immediate relief and prevent future flare-ups. You knew exactly what was wrong with them and exactly how to get them results.

You might as well be wearing a mask and a cape because, in that moment, you are their hero.

The cost for your therapy is $3,000.

So observing their pain do you just spring the $3,000 on them? "I see you're in pain and I know we just met . . . but I can fix it for $3,000!"

No. Of course you don't. You just met five minutes ago.

They have already forgotten your name and they don't trust you (yet). Not enough to fork over $3K, at least.

But what if you said, "I'm so sorry to hear that. You're clearly in pain. As luck would have it, I'm a back pain specialist. I own a clinic down the street. Would you like to [insert some small step that gets them a result and builds trust in themselves and in you]?"

Whether it's a free PDF they could read, a video series with exercises to help with pain, or a free consultation . . .

What's the next logical step that gets them from Point A to Point B? Notice how I didn't say from Point A to Point Z? Then, after trust has been built and you know what you're doing, what's the next step? Do you have a $30 supplement, lotion, or treatment you could sell them? What about a series of three therapy visits to your office?

Would you agree that after getting them results and building trust in your method that *now* would be an appropriate time to invite them into your breakthrough treatment for $3,000?

That's what I mean when I say your "Ideal Sales Process."

If you're a car dealer you want people to come onto your car lot, meet a sales rep, take a test drive, negotiate on the price, talk to financing, and buy the car along with the maintenance and warranty program.

If you're a coach or consultant you'd want people to read your book, watch your training, get on a strategy session, and sign up for your services.

If you're a dentist, it's a cleaning, then whitening, braces, and finally cosmetic dentistry and having them come back every six months like clockwork.

Why Funnels?

A funnel is simply the step-by-step, hold-your-hand approach to transforming a total stranger into a repeat buyer.

Put that way, there's a 99% chance you already have a funnel in your business and you just don't know it.

It's your ideal sales process, mapped out step-by-step online.

It's called a funnel because of the shape that it takes as people go through your process.

Back to the car dealer:

On a busy Saturday 1,000 people visit your lot. One hundred want to go on test drives. Twenty-five of those people talk to financing and ten people buy a car. Three buy the extended care plan.

That busy coffee shop? Two hundred people enter and buy something. One hundred spend more (larger drink, add shots). Fifty add food to their coffee order. Two people buy the $500 espresso machine while they wait in line.

Online business? One thousand visitors hit your training registration page and 300 people give you their email address. One hundred show up and ten buy your product. Of the ten that buy, three take your up-sell (more on that later).

**For this funnel diagram go to
onehourfunnel.com/resources

"I already have a website … why do I need a funnel?"

Think of your website like a brochure. It's necessary since so much of business is done online. Its highest use is to build trust and authority in you and your brand.

But it's a lousy salesperson.

If you had a salesperson in your company that only handed out brochures, they wouldn't last until the lunch break. They'd be out of a job!

That's why you need a funnel.

It's the hold-your-hand approach to taking a total stranger through your ideal sales process.

If your business were a clothing retailer at the mall (malls are still a thing, right?) you'd want them to welcome shoppers in, show them what's on sale (build trust), help them choose outfits, and eventually get them to apply for your store credit card (up-sell).

Russell Brunson, the CEO and one of the co-founders of the software ClickFunnels, says that businesses "only need a funnel if they want more leads and more sales!"

I couldn't have said it better myself.

Now that you see how a funnel works, you'll notice that funnels are everywhere. In these last few pages we've talked about car dealers, clothiers, coffee shops, back pain clinics, dentists, and more.

Ever see a coupon for that new restaurant that popped up in town? Redeem the coupon (free front-end offer that builds trust) and BOOM … you're in their funnel. They can add you to their email list, up-sell you wine, apps, drinks and desserts, and invite you back for lunch the next day or casually show you their catering menu.

You've gone from a total stranger to this establishment to now ordering the sandwich tray for thirty-two of your co-workers!

What a Funnel IS and What it ISN'T

We now know that a funnel IS the best way to get more leads and customers and to grow your business.

BUT a funnel ISN'T a magical golden goose that can never fail for your business.

The truth is a funnel that works can take a long time and can be expensive. A friend of mine charges $100,000 for a funnel...plus *equity* in your company!

That's why I made the One Hour Funnel system. I've built hundreds of funnels for myself and for clients and developed a process that allows me to quickly build high-converting, profitable funnels in any niche in only an hour.

The rest of this book will show you exactly how I do this in a short amount of time every time.

Welcome to the One Hour Funnel™!

Part One
PLAN IT

CHAPTER 1
KNOW YOUR MARKET

D o you ever feel like you're in the wrong place?

Have you ever been surrounded by people (in person or online) that aren't like you? Or conversations are going on that you're either disinterested in, don't understand, or find offensive?

On Sundays during the summer (in that dreaded sports-lovers lull between professional basketball ending and football kicking off) my family will watch golf.

Technically, we'll have golf on the TV while we go about our other household buzz. And in-between drawing and chores and wrestling with my three sons, sometimes I'll catch the commercials and think to myself, *I'm not their target market.*

They're advertising high-end watches (my last watch was a red plastic watch from a discount store), Cadillacs, Buicks, and retirement homes.

I will probably never buy a Buick and I'm not planning on retiring to Florida anytime soon.

I'm not the right market.

(Side note, this is why I love Facebook advertising as compared to TV, print, and radio. You can get super targeted. More on that later).

In March of 2018 I went to the Funnel Hacking Conference in Orlando. This event brings together thousands of people that want to run better businesses, get better results, want more leads and sales, and want to leverage the latest marketing and advertising efforts to grow their company using sales funnels.

Every speaker was awesome. I felt like I was in the right spot.

I felt like the event was made just *for me.*

That's how you want *your* prospect to feel.

You want them to feel like you custom-tailored your product or service for *them.*

Then, once we know the market, we craft irresistible offers and show them to our prospects. It's that simple and it's that hard.

The Role of Marketing

The role of marketing in your business is to move your prospects and customers seamlessly and subtly through each step of your customer journey—where they go from total stranger to referring others to you.

Notice I didn't say, "bait and switch your prospects," "trick them," "pounce on them when they're vulnerable," or "move them faster than they're willing to go with the latest persuasion tactics."

That's no way to build a lasting relationship. Sure, you'll make some money and some sales but you'll be exposed by a lack of internal systems and quality fulfillment that will only cause your refunds to go higher and your reputation to go lower.

When we set our eyes on the goal of building a lasting relationship with each person we meet, it changes every conversation along the way.

Our focus will be on value, transforming their lives, and getting results for them. We want people to have a better life or whatever our desired outcome is for them: more time, freedom, money, peace, relationships, etc.

Put more simply, we want to take people from a sad "before" state to a happy "after" state.

They have pain in their life that they want to alleviate and it's our job to make them happy.

The Dinner Party

When we moved to Colorado in 2004, my wife and I knew exactly two people. Luckily, those two people knew a bunch of other people and in no time we had a small network of new friendships.

One of the ways we quickly cultivated those relationships was by having small dinner parties at our house.

You know the type...

You break out the nice dishes and flatware (the ones from your wedding you keep in the closet), light a scented candle, pick up the mess around the house, sweep the porch, and cook a nicer dinner than normal.

Why do we go to so much trouble when we host someone in our home?

Simple. We want them to feel welcome, like we were

planning for them. We want them to feel comfortable and know that we want the new relationship to get off on the right foot.

Bonus points in the digital age: you can go to their LinkedIn or Facebook profile and learn about them. Where'd they grow up? Do they have kids or pets? And what are their names? What line of work are they in? What are their favorite foods?

This sets the table for a natural conversation during your first interaction.

How We Get This Wrong In Our Own Business

What does this have to do with marketing our products?

1. **We don't prepare.** Have you ever clicked on an ad or walked into a business and they weren't ready for you? The other day I walked into a higher-end hipster coffee shop and no one was behind the counter. I craned my neck over the pastry display and saw the lone worker on her phone watching YouTube videos. Oops. It left me feeling like they weren't expecting me and weren't ready to serve me.

    Back to that Funnel Hacking Conference ... when I got near the convention hall to register I was high-fived no less than eight times by enthusiastic conference volunteers. Registration took about forty-two seconds, which is crazy fast considering there were thousands of attendees. I got my badge, shirt, and tote bag and the conference started right on time. I knew how much planning and work had gone into that amazing experience at the event and had a great time. Now I'm a customer for life and I'm telling you about it.

2. **We don't listen.** Nothing is worse than feeling misunderstood. Do your customers feel like they're shouting into a black hole? We hand them our "thing" and they say, "I don't want this ... you're not listening to me!"

   A great way to listen is to join the conversations already happening. I'm part of several (paid and free) Facebook groups with other business owners in various niches. I make a habit to spend fifteen minutes a day in each group to see what people are commenting on, questions they're asking, and what they're complaining about.

   Whenever possible, I add value and answer their questions.

   One group I was in had a ton of chatter over a week around webinars (online presentations to teach, sell, and engage). People were getting so stuck with the flow of a successful webinar. So one day I whipped up a quick template to give away in that group and people were head-over-heels with gratitude.

   And, naturally, my status and influence in that group grew and I am now seen as a leader in that group.

   I don't care what niche you're in or what market you serve. Your prospects and customers are already having conversations online. It's your job to join in and add value.

3. **We don't serve.** I'm assuming you're in business (or considering starting a business) because you've figured something out. You took a pain point and solved it; saw a gap in the market and filled it. There's some mystery in the world around your product/service and people think it's hard. But to you, it's easy.

   So you hung your shingle out and opened the doors.

   Now it's your job to serve your customers and get them an actual result. Either teach them how (do-it-yourself or DIY), take their hand and show them how (done-with-you or DWY), or just do it for them.

How to Know Your Market

Okay, so we need to prepare for our customers, listen to their concerns, and actually serve them.

But how do we know the market, get inside their heads, and make great products and services for them?

I developed a framework called "The 5 Fs."

> **Go to onehourfunnel.com/resources to download the diagrams and resources for this book

1. Who is it **FOR**?

   Is your product for single moms? Is it for aspiring photographers in their 20s? Is it for military veterans that love to work out? Is it for empty-nesters that love to bake?

   In this section, be as specific as possible. What type of industry are they in? Is your product better suited for people of a certain age, gender, or part of the country? Do they have any common interests or activities?

Spend 3–5 minutes brainstorming your ideal customer.

2. How do they **FEEL?**

    What's an average day like for your new customer? What emotions do they feel in a day? Are they ambitious, calm, annoyed, harried, busy, overwhelmed, or always in zen-mode?

    Do they have lots of down time? Are they active? Do they love to learn?

    Spend 3–5 minutes brainstorming how your ideal customer feels.

    Pro tip: Remember those Facebook groups you're a part of now? The ones where you're listening and adding value? Just ask them. Use a question like *As a [person in this group], do you ever feel like [perceived pain point or emotion they're feeling]?*

3. What do they find **FRUSTRATING?**

    You may have already answered this in Step Two, but if not, spend a minute and answer it now.

    What friction points do your prospects have in their lives and how can you alleviate them?

    For example, if I had invented the Keurig and I was trying to replace old cheap traditional coffee makers, I'd focus on those frustrations:

    Tired of asking your whole household how much coffee they want? You have to try to find the missing measuring scoop, fill the water in the pot and pour it in the tank, throw out the disgusting messy filter from the day before, carefully pour the grounds in the filter, brew twelve cups of coffee (which takes fourteen minutes), and then you find out you guessed wrong on the quantity and then it goes stale! You have to reheat it until it's undrinkable and then throw it out …

My blood pressure rises just thinking of those days.

Now I pour water into the reservoir once a week, cleanly place a plastic cup in the brewer and it brews a consistent cup of coffee each time in less than thirty seconds. No mess. No hassle.

No more frustrations.

Consider your market and spend five minutes writing down what they find frustrating.

4. Who do they **FOLLOW**?

Everyone is influenced by someone. It might be a book, movie, author, TV show, "guru," or event.

The cool thing about paying attention to who your prospect follows is two-fold.

One, you can follow that person and join the conversation. Learn the jargon and slang associated with that influencer.

Ever walked into a group conversation where everyone is talking about Episode 136 of Season 11 of a show you've never seen or heard of? That's like joining a book club and never reading the book. You don't know what's going on.

Second, whenever we want to advertise our product

or service we have a baked in market segment. If your entire target market listens to a certain podcast, reads a particular blog, or goes to the same event, it makes our lives so much easier. We can either advertise, sponsor, co-host, or contribute to that conversation.

Simply put, if you have a natural health remedy and you want to give away free samples, you'd be smart to advertise on Dr. Josh Axe's blog or target his audience on Facebook. His people are *your* people.

Spend 5–10 minutes writing down people, authors, teachers, leaders, events, books, and magazines that your target customers follow.

5. What's their **FINISH LINE**?

Would you watch a football game if it didn't have any rules? Would you pay attention if no score was kept and it was just over whenever the referee felt like it? That wouldn't be very satisfying, would it?

What if I ran into you on the street and said "Hey, come with me. We're gonna run in this race!" You'd probably want to know the rules of the race, the length, and where you'd end up when you're done.

If I'm selling you on how to bake a cake, the finish line is when you take a big bite of moist, sumptuous cake.

If I'm selling you a lead-generating funnel, the finish line is a traffic-ready online asset, meaning that you'd send traffic to it and it would do its job of converting traffic to leads and leads to sales.

If I'm selling you a custom-knit scarf in my online store, the finish line is a warm neck in the winter.

If I'm selling a coaching program to help you meet the love of your life, the finish line is getting you a date.

What result are we promising them at the end, and how will we know when we're done?

In other words, how will we tell them what we're going to do, actually do it, and look at it and say, "It's done! We did it!"

Take three minutes and clearly articulate the finish line for your customer.

CHAPTER 2
MONETIZE YOUR OFFER

R emember that the goal of our product or service is to articulate the transformation from the unhappy, sad "before state" to a satisfied and happy "after state."

The greater the transformation, the greater the results, and the more money we can charge.

Take the health and fitness niche, for example.

If your goal was to get in the best shape of your life, and I claimed I could help you lose one pound in a week, how much money would you give me? How much is that "transformation" worth to you?

Arguably nothing. Zero dollars and zero cents. The transformation is too insignificant and small.

But what if I helped you lose 100 pounds, get ripped, be on the cover of magazines, and turn your life completely around? How much is that worth? $10,000? $100,000? Priceless?

Gary Vaynerchuk, social media mogul and influencer, wanted to get in better shape. He tried half-heartedly on his own with no results and eventually did something drastic.

He hired a personal trainer to move in with him. This dude woke him up, went to the gym with him, cooked his meals, and monitored every facet of his life. He travelled to conferences and speaking events so that Gary wouldn't deviate from the plan.

I don't know what Gary paid this trainer, but I know that Gary got in the best shape of his life. His business, already strong, flourished even more now that Gary was in top shape.

If you're already in business (or thinking of starting one) you probably already have a core way you get results for people. It could be your coaching, IT services, software, supplement, physical product, or whatever business you're in.

Great. Let's call that a "core offer." It's your flagship product/service that you give someone in exchange for their money.

If you simply craft a core offer without giving your prospects additional ways to engage with you, you could be leaving a lot of money on the table. Here's why ...

The Value Journey

The value journey is simply the steps you take with someone to get them from a complete stranger to where they won't shut up about how awesome you are.

To maximize the transformation we help them achieve (and what we can charge) we're going to map out 3–5 levels of service we can provide at varying price points.

Bear in mind there is no right answer here; we are going to get your brain going on how to seamlessly and subtly move people through the process of working with you.

What is your core offer? Take a minute to jot it down on the worksheets provided at onehourfunnel.com/resources.

Now we use a technique called "splintering" to come up with other cheaper offers. These offers won't get people the most transformation, but that's not the point at this step in the process.

It's about momentum and progress towards their finish line.

Imagine you're selling me the idea of going to Hawaii—my favorite place on the planet.

You'd highlight the snorkeling, relaxation, hammocks, beaches, weather, and making memories with my family.

You'd probably leave the part out about the airport parking, the crowded shuttle bus, long lines, taking my shoes off, checked baggage fees, missed connections, and lack of leg room for my 6' 3" frame.

Remember to focus on the finish line.

Now, there are a few ways you can get me to Hawaii . . .

First off, I could figure it out on my own. It would take forever (hitchhike from Colorado to California, then swim or row a boat to Hawaii), and it would be dangerous. But it would be cheap!

Next, I could fly commercial. Safer, faster, but still not very comfortable.

At the top would be flying private. Everything is tailored to me. Maximum comfort, convenience, and cost.

Regardless of the method I choose, I'm still getting to Hawaii. All that changes is the speed, comfort, and price it takes to get me there.

We're building your business the same way; crafting different offers to get them the same results at varying price points and levels of involvement on your end.

Why Is It Called a Funnel?

Ever wondered why online marketing is referred to as a funnel?

Let's say that you have 1,000 people come to your website where you offer a free report.

Three hundred (30%) take the bait in exchange for their email address. Of those 300, you make an offer to join a paid program that gets them a quick result for $49. Thirty people take you up on it (10%).

Now of those thirty, you extend an invitation into your core offer. Another 10% take you up on your offer at $1,500.

You turned 1,000 visitors into 300 email subscribers, 30 customers at $50, and 3 at $1,500 each.

When you draw it out, it looks like a funnel. A visual can be found at the resources page located at onehourfunnel.com/resources.

Splintering

Let's take some action. We're going to splinter your core offer.

Not sure where to start? If your core offer is delivered one-on-one, could you do a group model (one-to-many) for less money? People still get a result, but it's not as expensive and not as personalized.

What if we splintered it again? What would need to happen for your product/service if they could do it on their own? Similar to this book, I'm bundling everything I know about marketing and funnels and putting it into this book. I could charge $10,000+ for the funnels in my agency, or I could show you the exact road map in this book and you can do it on your own.

Make sense?

The Value Ladder

Russell Brunson from ClickFunnels describes this process as the Value Ladder.

On the front end is some "bait"—something the market really wants. It could be a free trial, report, PDF, cheat sheet, gift certificate, or discount.

The role of the bait is to convert traffic to a lead and bring them into your world so you can help them get a result.

When they take the bait, then we can make them an offer to convert them from a lead/subscriber to a customer. We want them to take their credit card out of their wallet and give us some amount of money.

There are a lot of ways to do that, too many to describe in this book. Join the free Facebook group located on the resources page at onehourfunnel.com/resources for more ideas.

From there, we ascend them to our core offering.

Service Business

Bait	Coupon for carpet cleaning one room
Low-Ticket	Clean their carpet for an amount of money
Core Offer	Clean all the rooms in their home

Supplements

Bait	Free sample
Low-Ticket	30-day supply
Core Offer	"Stack" of supplements; auto-ship

Coaching/Consulting

Bait	Free PDF/Cheat sheet about your industry
Low-Ticket	Paid training, book, or resource
Core Offer	Eight-week program

Fitness

Bait	Free personal training session
Low-Ticket	Paid challenge
Core Offer	Package of training sessions

Dentist

Bait	Free teeth whitening
Low-Ticket	Cleaning
Core Offer	Cosmetic dentistry/orthodontics

Are you getting this? Isn't this cool?

Remember, a funnel is just the step-by-step, hold-your-hand approach you want to take someone through.

Take five minutes and write out your Value Ladder (a.k.a. your funnel) on the provided worksheets.

At this point, focus on the results at a high level and don't get bogged down in the mechanism. Trust me, we'll get there later.

CHAPTER 3
THE MAP

The Napkin Project

One of the first marketing courses I took was by Ryan Deiss of Digital Marketer. It was called the Napkin Project and the basic premise was that he mapped out his hugely successful business on a cocktail napkin.

It's that simple.

At this point you know your market and have your monetization strategy mapped out. Use a whiteboard or a napkin or a super cool free mapping tool that I love called Funnelytics (funnelytics.io) to map out your flow.

Congratulations, you now have the framework for your One Hour Funnel™!

Part Two
SAY IT

CHAPTER 4
SPECIALIZATION

I'm going to let you in on a little secret...

Y ou may protest at first, but it's true (and your vote doesn't count at the moment)...

Ready? Here it is:

YOU are the ONLY one that can take YOUR message to the market!

Thinking that you can't do something because someone else did it is the #1 killer of great ideas.

I saw a YouTube video (available on the resources page) about the richest place on Earth. It's not Shanghai, New York City, or Dubai...

It's the graveyard. In the graveyard there are songs that have never been composed, poems never written, and businesses never launched.

So the next time you think *I can't do ___, because so-and-so already does it and he/she is famous!* I want you to know that it's not true.

I know how you feel because I used to believe the same thing.

I let the fear hold me back from starting The One Hour Funnel™.

From making a course ...

From starting my podcast ...

From writing this book ...

I would think, *Ryan Deiss already teaches online marketing. And Russell Brunson is the funnel guy ...*

Lie after lie, suppressing my ideas and selfishly keeping them hidden. Do you ever feel that way?

Just think, while I was too afraid to share my expertise with the world, how many people could I have helped?

So as you consider your expertise, your genius, your gift that you've been given to put out into the world ...

Just remember that YOU are the only one with *your* background, *your* life experiences, and *your* stories that shape who you are.

I don't care if Brendon Burchard has done it. Or Oprah hosted an episode about it. Or Gary Vee made a YouTube video about your idea. Or if whoever you admire most wrote a blog about it.

You're YOU. They're THEM.

Now that we've cleared that up ...

Remember When?

Do you remember where you were when you had the dream for your product, service, or idea? Maybe you were at a conference, a networking event, mastermind, or listening to a podcast while on a walk.

You were going along with life, minding your own business, then the idea hit you like a bolt of lightning.

If you're like me, you got really excited about your idea and shared it with those closest to you. You ran to secure the domain name and the Twitter handle and stayed up all night sketching out the business plan and prototypes. You scoured the internet to see if anyone was doing something similar and, for bonus points, you may have even done a trademark search on Google.

Remember that moment?

That's called your epiphany moment.

An epiphany is defined as "a new grasp of reality through a simple, striking event" and "an illuminating discovery or realization."

In our quest to stand out above the noise, the epiphany is our origin story. It's our "why."

In his book *Expert Secrets*, Russell Brunson describes an epiphany as "simply a story that takes someone through the emotional experience that got YOU excited about the new opportunity you're presenting to them." To find out how to get a free copy of this book head over to the resources page at onehourfunnel.com/resources.

Take a few minutes and recall that moment when you got your idea.

Where were you? Who were you with? What did an average day look like for you? Finish this sentence, "Once upon a time..."

Then what happened? Finish this transition statement, "Suddenly..."

I came up with the idea for the One Hour Funnel™

after talking to entrepreneurs that were tired of spending money on developers, getting stuck in techno-hell, and letting their ideas die. So I created a system where they can get high-converting, traffic-ready funnels made in only an hour of their time.

In a sentence: I created the One Hour Funnel™ to help busy entrepreneurs take back control of their marketing.

My wife, Christy, has an event planning company that specializes in helping seven-figure entrepreneurs host profitable two-day workshops. Her epiphany came about after seeing successful business owners lose touch with their core clientele in an overly automated online world.

Isn't that awesome?

Brainstorm what your epiphany statement is and write it on the provided worksheets located at onehourfunnel.com/resources.

CHAPTER 5
TRANSFORMATION

It's only about transformation.

S ome businesses thrive on before and after photos. The latest diet or workout gadgets come to mind. Those are helpful because they are so visual.

In 2015 I started taking my fitness more seriously. Dad-bod was a reality and one day I found myself on a scale with the blue LED lights declaring 243 pounds. Easily the heaviest I had ever been.

So I hired a coach and stepped way out of my comfort zone and signed up for a fitness competition that meant shaved body hair, spray tan, the whole deal.

Long story short, over the sixteen weeks, I lost exactly 50 pounds and the before/after photos are crazy! You can read the whole story over at howtobeafitdad.com.

Our business is the same way. Remember that the primary function of our marketing and storytelling is to take someone from the sad "before" state to a happy "after" state.

Remember the epiphany from the previous chapter? We want to use transformation stories to help people that are on the fence about working with us picture what life would be like after they're done experiencing our product or service.

Make sense?

And back in Chapter 2 (Value Ladders) remember that the bigger transformations we can provide, the more we can charge for our products/services.

The most common way to do this is with case studies. People love to read case studies.

They're secretly thinking to themselves, *Will this program work for me?* The more clearly they can picture themselves in our transformation stories, the easier it will be to sell our services.

If you have success stories, turn those into case studies. Reach out to those customers and ask if they'd shoot a quick video or write a story about their life *before* they worked with you and now what life is like *afterward*.

Notice I didn't say "get a testimonial"? Testimonials are fine but typically don't turn out the way you want them to.

I conducted a soft launch in a beta group in February 2018 for my One Hour Funnel™ course and at the end asked for testimonials. I got a lot of "Cody is a great guy and super smart!" and "No one cares about your business more than Cody."

Flattering…but not exactly what I needed to help other people picture themselves succeeding with my program.

Once I asked for transformation stories I got this:

"This course takes the headache out of figuring out what to say and do and where to put everything . . . it's a step-by-step process . . . Without this, I would spend hours working on my funnel, only to watch it spiral out of control . . ."

"I would highly recommend the One Hour Funnel System to anyone who was lost like I was in the world of digital marketing. I literally knew nothing about funnels when I began the course and then halfway through, I had acquired so much knowledge that I started a new side company selling the information in my brain and using Cody's methodology to put it to market."

"This is a total game changer. I'm able to get the funnel pages going much quicker, and now I know what to say and where to say it so it creates interest in what I have to say. Thanks for helping me understand how to do that. I have my ads going, and I'm already starting to get new leads and I know that it's going to lead to an influx of new business."

Big difference.

If you're just starting and don't have some case studies then you need to go get some. Do some work for free or cheap and let them know that you need a case study for your product, service, or idea. Then capture them and use them in your marketing.

The Transformation Framework
Let me break it down further for you:

1. Acknowledge The Present Situation
2. Share Your Epiphany
3. What They'll Experience WITH Your Product
4. What The Future Is Like WITHOUT Your Product
5. Invitation/Call to Action

Simple, right? Here's how it would look in one of your funnel pages:

Acknowledge Present Situation:
"Being an entrepreneur is tough... between selling, fulfilling, accounting, and team management it can feel overwhelming. The last thing you want to do is spend weeks of time and thousands of dollars getting all your ideas to the marketplace."

Epiphany
"That's why I created the One Hour Funnel™, a simple system to create high-converting funnels in only an hour of your time."

Life WITH It
"With it, you can take back the most crucial element of your business—your marketing. Imagine spending only an hour of your time and having a lead-generating funnel."

Life WITHOUT It

"Without it, you'll never actually be in control of the life blood of your business and will spend long nights and week-ends (and a heap of cash) bringing revenue-generating ideas to life."

Invitation

"Go to onehourfunnel.com/get-started to sign up!"

Take ten minutes and fill out the Transformation work-sheet so you can quickly get people to picture themselves succeeding with your product or service.

CHAPTER 6
INVITATION

"I made this for you!"

If you bumped into a stranger on a crowded street, holding a plate of cookies and shouted, "I MADE THESE FOR YOU!" they would pepper spray you.

That's creepy.

You don't run up to people and shove things in their face.

In the dating world, this would be like meeting a woman in your small group, gym, or the local bar and proposing marriage with no more relationship equity than awkward eye contact.

You'd get slapped or pepper sprayed.

So often in marketing we jump to the sale. We take strangers off the internet and shove our products in their face. We skip all the steps and go right in for the kill.

You might get lucky and make a few sales, but it's no way to have a lasting relationship (in life or in business).

Now, on the other hand, what if we invite someone into our home? We take their coat, pour them a glass of wine, use the nice silverware, have a nice meal … and then bring them the same plate of cookies and place them in front of them and say, "Here … I made these for you!" Odds are somewhere in the neighborhood of 100% they'd take one (or this is when *you* get to pepper spray *them*).

When we add value in advance and tell great stories of successful transformation, people start to think, *I like this company. They get me and they make products or services for* me.

At this point in the relationship they are practically begging to work with you.

So we tell them how to work with us.

Buy Now. Schedule a Call. Yes, I Want This!

I was reviewing a funnel page for someone that came through my freefunnelfeedback.com/home website. He was a real estate broker. Let's call him Trent (actual name changed to protect the innocent).

His call-to-action button on his site, in 100-point font said "YES! TRENT PLEASE!" and then in super tiny 12-point font it said "I NEED YOUR HELP."

Aside from the design being horrible, I had no idea what was on the other side of that button. Turns out it was a calendar scheduling tool.

So don't do that.

Here are a few tips to improve your funnel pages.

Have a very clear call to action. Go to onehourfunnel.com/home for a live example. At the time of this writing I have a big orange button that says "Sign Up For Free Training" on the top right-hand side.

Make the call-to-action button a different color than

the primary colors on your site. For example: green, blue, or orange.

Make sure it's at the very top right of your page, as well as above the fold. The "fold" is a term taken from the newspaper world and refers to the content of your page before someone has to scroll down.

Part Three

DO IT

CHAPTER 7
CONSTRUCT

T he developer for our suburban neighborhood in Colorado Springs decided against putting fences between the yards. One backyard flows into another; property lines are punctuated by rocks, mulch berms, and spruce trees.

As our three boys were getting older, we grew tired of them wandering into yards four houses down. One summer we decided to put up a privacy fence.

I'm not very handy but wanted to do the project myself, so we brought in the big guns: my father-in-law, Mike, and his brother Bob, who happens to be a general contractor.

We sketched it out, drew the property lines, planted the posts deep in concrete, cut a power line (oops!), fixed the power line, put up the cross beams, and then nailed in the pickets. All told it took two long, sweaty days.

We looked at the work of our hands and slapped each other on the back with a sigh that said, "We did it!"

We mapped out the plan, assembled the materials,

and put up a beautiful fence so our boys could play safely in their new confines.

I think that's why I love building funnels so much.

With a push of a few buttons you go from *idea* to *implemented*.

If you've done the work in the first two sections, you now have permission to move forward with your funnel building. And if you haven't done the work yet, go back and do it with the provided worksheets. Not only will it give you extreme clarity on the entire process, but it will make Part Three feel like a walk in the park.

Let's check in and see where we are:

1. You're clear on your **MARKET**: who you serve and how you serve them.
2. You have your **MONETIZATION** strategy: what you will give this market in exchange for money.
3. You have a **MAP**: the flow of your customer journey from stranger to referring your business.
4. You're clear on your **SPECIALIZATION**: why you're the unique person to take your message to the market.
5. You know how to provide and communicate **TRANSFORMATION**: getting results for the people you serve and telling others about it.
6. You consistently extend an **INVITATION** to your market and invite them to work with you.

The last three stops on our journey are *Construct, Connect,* and *Confirm.*

The Technology

There are lots of amazing technologies out there that you can use to build your marketing funnels. For the sake of this book (and my entire business) I'm going to focus on ClickFunnels. However, you're free to use whatever technology you choose.

I love ClickFunnels because it lays out the entire sales process in a linear fashion. I used to use other software but would get everything confused on the order of Step One, Step Two, etc. The links were going all over the place and I couldn't make it work like I wanted it to.

I've been using online funnels for many years, and when ClickFunnels came along I knew it had changed the game. It had magically fixed all the shortcomings of other page building software out there.

Note: I made custom, special funnel templates just for readers of this book. To grab those, along with a 14-day free trial of ClickFunnels, go to onehourfunnel.com/resources. Test it out for a few weeks and see if it's for you. Either way, keep the templates with my compliments.

The Old Way

When I built the funnel for How to Be a Fit Dad back in 2015, I used a Wordpress plugin. Though it was affordable, it was impossible to use. I couldn't see my modifications in real time. I would change a headline, picture, resize a video, or change the layout then I had to publish it to see the changes.

If I didn't like it and wanted to change it I had to go back to the editor and modify the page and publish all over again. It took forever and it was really frustrating.

Even worse, I couldn't keep the pages straight. If you've ever used Wordpress, you know how having multiple pages can get really messy on the back end.

The New Way

Use ClickFunnels and use the templates I provide at onehourfunnel.com/resources. You can plug and play everything from the worksheets and have your funnel up in *way less* than an hour.

Three Core Funnels

Remember that the point of our marketing is to build a relationship from a total stranger to someone who is referring your company. Just like a relationship, it can't happen overnight. If you meet someone and want to get married, there's a sequence and measure you take them through to end up at the altar.

You can build a huge business using these three funnels alone.

One funnel is used to turn cold traffic into leads, then offer them the lower ticket item on your value ladder.

One is used to convert people who are on the fence into your core offer.

The last one is used to get people into a higher-ticket (profit-maximizing) offer.

Let's go through these step-by-step to see how they work in your business.

Funnel #1: The Lead Generator Funnel

I first met my wife, Christy, when we were in 8th grade at church camp. It was definitely not love at first sight (we were awkward junior high students). We only saw each other two times per year at camp events, but we stayed in touch and created a strong emotional bond through email and letters.

I remember, though, when everything changed in senior year.

I was at the same church camp, in the same chapel waiting for service to begin when the doors flung wide and the most beautiful woman I had ever seen walked into the chapel in slow motion. A gentle breeze blew her wavy brown hair back while a dove descended and perched on her shoulder...

Okay, my memory is a little fuzzy seeing it was almost twenty years ago, but that's how I remember it.

In all seriousness, she was tan, fit, and her long brown hair and light-blue dress were unforgettable. She came to me and asked if we could sit together.

I was transfixed... but I didn't propose to her that night.

No, that would come almost three years later...

Generally speaking, you don't go from "visually captivated" to "married" in one move.

That's what this first funnel is like. You take a total stranger, introduce yourself, add value to them, get them a quick win, and then you have permission to continue to cultivate the relationship.

The Lead Generator Funnel is perfect for generating leads, growing your email list, selling them low-ticket offers (also known as converting traffic into a buyer), and introducing them to your organization and brand.

Here's how it works:

1. Traffic (i.e. viewers or visitors) hits your landing page. This page has a little bit of information but is very focused on one main goal: encourage the visitor to opt-in for your lead magnet, which is your freebie at the bottom of your value ladder. This is typically via an email address but can also be via a Facebook Messenger Bot.

2. Once they enter their name and email address, they are taken to your low-ticket offer on the next page in your funnel. This page has a few elements. The first is a headline acknowledging their previous action ("Thank you for requesting the [FREE REPORT] ... it will be in your email inbox in about five minutes. Before you go—watch this video ..."). Then, via a video or text (or both) you tell them about your offer. Remember that it should be complementary and the next logical step in the funnel. That means if they opted in for a free book, then you can sell them the audio recordings and a master class training about the contents of the book. If you give away a free makeup brush then the next step can be a sampler of your core makeup products.

3. If they take you up on your offer, then the next page is an order form where they enter their payment details.

4. The last step is a Thank You page that tells them exactly what to expect next. For example, you'll send them directions on how to access a digital product or talk about the shipping of a physical product.

> ** To see a diagram of this funnel and a free template, go to the resources page at onehourfunnel.com/resources.

Funnel #2: The Webinar Funnel

If the Lead Magnet Funnel is "can I have your number?" then this funnel is "let's go on a date or two."

As the relationship matures, you start to spend more time together (assuming you like each other). You might do a day trip together, or *gasp* bring your date home to meet the family eventually.

In Funnel Land we take warm traffic that has engaged with our free content and further the relationship.

The Webinar Funnel is a great mechanism to use to sell a higher-ticket product to warm traffic, which are people that are starting to know, like, and trust you.

The buyer for this product might need some training, education, or warming up to you and your brand. A great way to do this is by hosting a webinar. Think of a webinar as simply an online training or seminar that is either live or on-demand.

A webinar is a great place to send warm traffic to continue to build your relationship and then make them a great offer.

Here's how it works:

1. Page 1 is an opt-in page for your training. The entire point of this page is to get them to register for the training by entering their name and email address. You can add elements of social proof (testimonials) and tease the content with indirect bullet points of what you'll be teaching.

2. When they register, Page 2 is the confirmation. On this page it is very helpful to give them more content you want them to consume. This could be joining a Facebook group, downloading a PDF or worksheet, or watching some pre-training video.

3. Whenever you host your webinar, you need a place to send people to take you up on your offer. Option One for Page 3 is a sales page where they can learn more about your offer and buy it. You'll send webinar traffic here. Again, have testimonials and social proof on this page to beef up your offer and make it easy to check out. Option Two is if you're scheduling consultation calls from your webinar. Then this page would be a call-scheduling page where you embed an online calendar system.

4. If you use a sales page, then you'll need an order form and thank you page.

5. If you use a call strategy, then a simple thank you page will do and put any pre-call details on that thank you page.

** To see a diagram of this funnel and a free template go to the resources page at onehourfunnel.com/resources.

Funnel #3: The High-Ticket Funnel

Christy and I dated for a few years throughout college and *knew* we were going to get married. So I gathered all the money I had as a college senior and got her a diamond ring. I remember walking with her that night to a special place on campus and she asked why my hands were so cold (I was so nervous). I stammered something about gratitude and love and blessing and asked her to marry me.

I don't know why I was nervous. I had done all the right things—I cultivated the relationship along the years, built trust, and proved to her that I was worth committing to for the long haul. I knew she would say yes ...

In marketing, this is where we want our best prospects to end up. We want them to trust us with their time and money so we can help them transform their lives and their business.

How do we sell the items at the TOP of our value ladder that we mapped out in Chapter 2? We can't spring this on cold traffic; they don't know, like, or trust us yet.

After we've done a good job of warming them up, we use Funnel #3: The High-Ticket Funnel.

This funnel is perfect for whenever you need to sell a product/service over the phone. Product price points are typically over $2k for this type of funnel (depending on your market).

This funnel is also awesome to use as an ascension funnel, meaning you send your hottest traffic and best customers direct to this funnel to consume the content and book a strategy session and ascend them to your higher-ticket products.

Here's how it works:

1. Page 1 talks about the problem that you solve with this product/solution. You'll focus on how you can help them get great results and tell transformation stories of people just like them. The entire goal of this page is to get people to book a call with you via an application.

2. Page 2 is the application. This is important because you don't want to be on the phone with people that aren't qualified financially or emotionally to work with you. The framing of the call is important, too. Typically you want to avoid words like "Strategy Session," which screams "sales call" in certain markets. I firmly believe that every step of your marketing funnel should be valuable in and of itself. So regardless of if they buy on your call, it should be valuable. For that reason I call mine "Funnel Accelerator Calls." The promise is, on the call, we'll map out the best funnel for your needs and then I'll email you a map of that funnel. More often than not they will choose to move forward with me; but if they don't, at least they have a ton of clarity about the next step.

3. After the application, we send them to a page with your calendar embedded on it. They can schedule the time that works for them. Usually these calls are free, but if you charge them then the next step would be an order form (some scheduling apps like Schedule Once will let you take payment as well).

4. Then they're taken to a confirmation page when they book a call.

** To see a diagram of this funnel and a free template, go to the resources page at onehourfunnel.com/resources.

CHAPTER 8
CONNECT

I love to travel.

I grew up in Dallas, Texas and my mom worked for an airline when we were growing up. One of the perks of her job was being able to travel for almost nothing. I remember going all over the US and Cancun for an awesome trip when I was 12.

In 2006 I started a side hustle as a public speaker. It wasn't glamorous, but I got to see a lot of different cities and meet a lot of people. Nowadays I travel to events, workshops, and conferences and still love it. New hotels to visit, new things to learn, and new relationships to make.

And most importantly? New restaurants to try.

I've had lobster rolls in Maine, fish tacos in San Diego, and the best BBQ of my life in Georgia.

Now when I travel to events I look up the best restaurants ahead of time and plan accordingly.

Let me ask you a question: Have you ever been at a restaurant and they got your order totally wrong? Either they forget the way you wanted your steak cooked, or missed a substitution, or just got it flat-out incorrect? I've even sat at dinner with my family and everyone's plate came out but mine. They just forgot that I was there!

Somewhere between the server nodding at you with glassy eyes and a plate of food appearing before you, there was a communication breakdown.

Think about everything that has to go right.

You, the server, the chef, the sous chef, the expediter, back to the server...all have to communicate clearly with each other. If anyone drops the ball along the way, the whole thing gets messed up.

Your funnel is no different.

Have you ever opted-in for something and gone to a different page in the funnel that makes no sense? Or placed an order but it never arrived? Or given your email address to receive something by email that never comes?

We don't want that to happen.

Once you build out your funnel, it's time to connect it to the other services you'll be using in marketing your new product/service idea.

Watch out. This is where things can get tricky. Depending on the page builder you're using, there is often robust help documentation if you get stuck. The most common software often connect very easily, but if you use something more obscure that you custom-coded then you're going to have a rough go. Then again, if you custom-coded an email system, I'm sure you can figure out how to integrate it.

Okay, so what are we going to connect and why?

Facebook and Google

Last Mother's Day, like a good son, I ordered my mom flowers and sent them to her house in Texas. The flower service I used only delivered on certain days of the week, and the flowers they send are very fresh. If my mom wasn't home, they'd just leave the flowers to bake in the Texas heat and humidity on her hot stone front porch.

I had to make sure she was going to be home when they were delivered.

When I ordered the flowers, they sent me the tracking code for the shipping company. I could see when they left Peru (told you they were fresh) and arrived in the US. I knew the date, time, and city when they arrived at the shipping hub. Then I saw the next day when they were delivered to Dallas (a few hours from her home). Then, on the date of delivery, I was hitting refresh like a day trader checking stocks to make sure they arrived while she was there.

I got a text alert when they were delivered and signed for followed shortly by a gushing, grateful text from my mom.

I knew exactly what was happening at every step of the process.

That's why we want tracking in place for Google and Facebook. I'm not going to go into it too much in this book, but it's critical to place Google's and Facebook's tracking code on all pages of your funnel.

That way you know how far people got in your sales process and you can speak to them anywhere they are in that process.

For example, if the flowers made it from Peru to Nashville but not to Dallas, I knew whom to call.

Similarly, if someone visits your opt-in page but doesn't opt-in we can show them an ad that says, "Hey, did life get in the way? Come back and finish your enrollment in this [COOL THING]." That is a very different conversation than someone who is completely cold in the universe.

Also, if they opt-in for your free content but don't buy your offer, you can speak to them differently.

It's like we're putting people in "buckets" based on their behavior on our funnel pages.

Here are some possible buckets we could use in our marketing:

- Totally cold. No idea who we are and haven't visited our page
- Saw opt-in page but didn't opt-in
- Saw offer but didn't buy it
- Bought offer but didn't register for webinar
- Registered for webinar but didn't show up
- Considered registering for a breakthrough strategy call but didn't pick a time
- And so on...

To integrate Facebook tracking into your funnel solution just Google "Facebook pixel" and the landing page software you're using.

Similarly, if you use Google Analytics, you can add that code to each page of your funnel as well.

**If you're using ClickFunnels I can show you how to quickly do this over at the resources page: onehourfunnel.com/resources.

Email System

If I order steak at a restaurant the only thing I want to come out of that kitchen is a steak prepared exactly how I ordered it. I don't want a plate of chicken or fish, and I don't want to be forgotten or ignored.

Your funnel is the same.

If I put my email address in the opt-in form and you say I'll get a PDF in six minutes... I want a PDF emailed to me in six minutes. It is a small micro-commitment that builds trust.

When someone opts-in for your lead magnet or buys your product, we want to be able to follow-up with them via email.

There are a lot of email systems out there but I recommend Active Campaign. It's robust in its capabilities and affordable to start. Feel free to use whatever email system you're comfortable with: MailChimp, Constant Contact, Actionetics, Infusionsoft, Aweber, etc.

Payment System

"The machine ate my money!" When I was a kid we'd go to the local mini golf/adventure park. It was like Vegas for 6-year-olds.

There was always that one machine that ate your money. A line would quickly form at the register of 6-year-olds hopped up on sugar and over-sensitized by the neon lights demanding a refund of their twenty-five cents into their sticky palms.

You put your money in and you expect something to happen, right?

Ever get a dollar bill *finally* flat enough for a vending machine to accept it? The fluorescent light flickers in the hall of the hotel and you press C9 and wait anxiously for the bag of chips to roll forward and . . .

Nothing.

You look around for someone to help but decide that you don't want the judgment of buying junk food at 12:07 a.m. and go back to your room with empty hands and an empty stomach.

It's frustrating, right?

You want your funnel to make money. When I got my first client at the agency in 2017, they asked me how I wanted to get paid. I was like a deer in headlights—I hadn't even considered that yet. I had to setup an invoicing system with a credit card processor overnight.

Luckily, this is easier now than ever.

A great place to get started is either Stripe or Paypal. They have similar fees to process payments and then get you paid.

They are typically free to sign up and then they take a cut of your transactions that they process, typically around 3%.

Once you get your payment system setup, you connect it to the order forms in ClickFunnels or whatever system you're using.

CHAPTER 9
CONFIRM

Now that your funnel pages are configured and connected, the last step is to confirm that everything is working.

Testing is crucial—especially if you're spending money on traffic and the pages are broken or not functioning well.

This is like our pre-flight plan. When I fly, I take for granted the years of pilot training and the thousands of buttons, switches, and dials in the cockpit. I usually put my headphones in and pray that the person in front of me doesn't want to recline their seat in-flight.

While I'm resting comfortably (okay, awkwardly) in my seat waiting to be hurtled through the air at 400 miles per hour, the pilots are running an extensive checklist before going to the runway.

Luckily, our checklist isn't as long.

Here is my testing protocol for every new funnel I build for myself or for people in my program:

1. **Open up every funnel page in a browser tab.** I use Chrome, but you can use whatever you want.

2. **Test that the Facebook Pixel is firing correctly.** Use a free Chrome plugin called "Facebook Pixel Helper" to ensure that everything is working on each page of your funnel and if you're using Facebook Standard Events like "Complete Registration," "Lead," or "Purchase."

3. **Opt-in to your own email system.** Keep in mind you may need to use a different email address because some auto-responders won't recognize a new entry into the system if you use the same email address twice. Make sure you're added to the right segment/ list in your email system. Make sure you get the emails that you think you should get.

4. **Test everything on mobile.** Most funnel software will allow you to view your pages in mobile and on tablet. More than 50% of traffic to your page will likely be on mobile so make sure it looks great!

5. **Buy your stuff.** Buy everything you sell (all the up-sells and down-sells). Make sure your card gets charged (and refund yourself if you want). Make sure the money goes into your payment system (Stripe). Make sure you get the follow-up emails you want to send to buyers. Check to see if you're now in the right segmentation list in your email system.

6. **Book your call.** If you're using a calendar system, schedule a call. Make sure the call gets registered in your calendar and that you get the follow-up emails that you want to get.

7. **Test your webinar.** If you have a webinar as part of your funnel, register for it. Make sure you're in the right part of your email system and that you're getting the necessary emails. Make sure you're registered with the webinar system itself (GoToWebinar or Zoom, etc).

8. **Push all the buttons.** Check every link on every page and make sure it works. Make sure there aren't any dead buttons.

If you passed all the tests:

1. Celebrate! High five someone around you.

2. Share the Love! Post your funnel link in the Facebook group which can be found at this page: onehourfunnel.com/resources. Tag me in the post so I can see it and celebrate with you!

CONGRATULATIONS

Y ou now have the keys to my entire A-to-Z process of building high-converting funnels for your business. When you get into the flow, you'll find that going from idea to implementation is a very short process. It often takes me 30–40 minutes to get a funnel live from scratch.

You can take this information with you and go have a huge business!

Or, if you'd like to move faster with my help, turn the page to find out how to get this done in only one hour of your time.

WHAT TO DO NEXT

Here's how to get your funnel outlined and published in only an hour.

You already know what your funnel is about and how you'll use it. You've spent months or years dreaming about what it would look like to have a predictable flow of leads and sales into your business.

You have an idea for a product or service to take to the world and make a positive impact in the lives of your market.

The hard part can be pulling it out of your head and onto a group of actual funnel pages so the world can see it.

That's where my team and I come in. We help people just like you get your funnel published in as little as one hour of your time.

Step 1: We spend forty-five minutes on the phone together outlining and developing your funnel pages and copy chunks. We get a good feel for your voice and your brand and walk you through our proprietary framework.

Step 2: My team and I go to work to publish your funnel based on your design and input.

Step 3: We schedule a fifteen minute hand-off call to go over your funnel pages and make any final tweaks. Then we publish your high-converting traffic-ready funnel.

Most people think it takes a lot of money and months of time to get a funnel. Now you can get a funnel put out into the world and working for you in as little as one hour of your time.

If you'd like our help, just email hello@onehourfunnel.com or go to onehourfunnel.com/get-started and we'll take it from there.

Made in the USA
San Bernardino, CA
12 September 2018